# The Craft Driven Lodge

Macoy Publishing & Masonic Supply Co., Inc.
Richmond, VA

www.macoy.com

First Edition

Copyright – 2014 by Daniel D. Hrinko

ISBN 978-0-88053-108-5

Printed in the United States of America

# The Craft Driven Lodge

by
Bro. Daniel D. Hrinko

# FOREWORD

Dr. Daniel Hrinko is a passionate student of Speculative Freemasonry. I first met Dan in 2005 when we reviewed the program for the local reception for the Grand Master of Masons in Ohio. At that time, Dan was Master of Clark Lodge # 101 in Springfield, Ohio, President of his Masonic District, and I was the Grand Marshal of the Grand Lodge of Ohio.

In Dan, I met a Brother who was thorough, curious, passionate, and thoughtful. Through the years we have traveled on own paths in Freemasonry. While I searched for what I could give and get in Freemasonry, Dan searched the reasons why a member would give and why he would receive some benefit by being a Mason.

He has carried that thoughtfulness and need for knowledge into his various positions in Freemasonry as Worshipful Master of Clark Lodge No. 101 in Springfield, Ohio; as the first Worshipful Master of Arts and Sciences Lodge No. 792 in Columbus, Ohio; as a District Education Officer, and a District Deputy Grand Master.

When the idea for Arts and Sciences Lodge was being developed, I became involved as Deputy Grand Master. As the first Lodge of its type in Ohio, I wanted to make sure these very bright men did not follow a path that strayed from the Ancient Landmarks. I soon learned that my worries were unfounded.

As it turned out, I have had several great honors associated with the life of Arts & Sciences Lodge. In October, 2009, as my first official act as Grand Master, I handed a Dispensation to Dan empowering Arts and Sciences Lodge to work implementing of the ideas these Brothers had been developing over the previous 2 years. At that time, I had confidence that this Lodge would have a profound impact on Freemasonry in Ohio for years to come. At that time, I specifically directed Dan to "go forth and multiply."

During the subsequent year, I visited this Lodge under dispensation on several occasions and was always pleased with the quality and passion of the work I saw as these Brothers labored in the quarries.

In my last official act as Grand Master in October, 2010, I had the privilege to sign a Charter issued by the Grand Lodge of Ohio and handed it to Dan with the appreciation of a Grand Lodge which saw these men form a Masonic Lodge.

I am glad our Masonic paths crossed beginning in 2005. It has led to a wonderful relationship that has developed through Freemasonry. I have since learned that Dan and I served as Master of our respective lodges in the early 80's but had never crossed paths. I also learned that we were raised to the sublime degree of Freemasonry within one year of each other in the late 1970's. After getting to know Dan in these past few years, I wish I had known him then.

Dan is not only a passionate craftsman in Speculative Freemasonry, but he is an actual craftsman. Using no power tools and relying on traditional hand tools, Dan crafts 18th century bentwood and joined boxes, tables, writing desks, and exact reproductions of originals pieces of Museum art from the 18th century.

But more importantly, he is an accomplished Masonic writer and lecturer. I have listened to Dan give education programs to Lodges and Masons all over Ohio. His ability to convey his Masonic knowledge and his love for Masonry is unmatched. Now he has placed this love and knowledge into this book.

Fraternally,

Bro. Terry Wayne Posey,
Past Grand Master, Grand Lodge of Ohio

# Author's Notes

The concept of a Craft Driven Lodge emerged from the experience of forming Arts & Sciences Lodge No. 792 under the Grand Lodge of Ohio. When Masons from central Ohio began to gather to discuss what a Masonic experience in a Lodge could be, numerous ideas were brought forth from this free and open discussion. Everyone involved seem to share several opinions not the least of which was a sense of disappointment in the superficial treatment of the esoteric aspects of Freemasonry, the deeper meanings of symbolism, and the limited opportunity to discuss and explore these topics within a Tiled Lodge.

As we began to gather and discuss these matters, it became clear that we were following a process whereby every member involved was viewed as an equal partner in this project and that the directions, goals, and implementation would be driven by every person involved and, therefore, would be the responsibility of everyone involved.

The purpose of this volume is to set forth fundamental principles that are essential to the long-term health and well-being of any organization including Masonic Lodges. In addition, I will present a review of the process followed by this group of Brothers that eventually resulted in the formation of Arts & Sciences Lodge under the Grand Lodge of Ohio. The general concepts that drove this process, the actions taken by numerous members of this group, the decisions that were made, and the challenges of implementation will be presented to the reader.

It is hoped that you will understand the process presented here and see the application of these principles to your own situation be it an individual who is interested in bringing a different quality to the experience in his

Lodge, a group of officers wishing to help their Lodge become more energizing and relevant to their Masonic goals, or for a group of Brothers interested in starting with a clean slate and forming a new Lodge. In all cases, the fundamental principles of the Craft Driven Lodge concepts are equally applicable.

The Craft Driven Lodge is designed with the purpose of allowing Brothers to identify their particular interests, determine their particular resources, and empower them to create a Lodge experience that is to their liking without being tied to any particular set of actions, ceremonies, or even fundamental beliefs beyond those universal to Speculative Masonry across the globe. Brothers using this process are free to choose from the numerous practices that have been developed as part of Speculative Masonry across the ages and choose those elements that are most consistent with their vision of what a Lodge experience should be.

As in all cases, Lodges affiliated with Grand Lodges are bound by the Constitution, bylaws, and edicts of that Grand Lodge which, in some situations, may limit the choices available to them. It is hoped that a partnership can be formed between the Brothers embarking on this process and the Grand Lodge that will be a supportive, collaborative relationship permitting Freemasonry, in various forms, to be explored and practiced. It is under such circumstances that fertile ground for the long-term development of Speculative Masonry can be prepared.

I humbly submit that the information presented within this tome is not the fruits of my labor alone. In fact, my primary role has been that of participating in the discussions from its early days, facilitating the implementation of the Will of these Brothers as Arts & Sciences Lodge No. 792 was being formed, and recording this process as observed for the benefit of others with similar interests and desires.

To be truly accurate, the name of every member of Arts & Sciences Lodge No. 792 as well as numerous other individuals who provided ideas and inspiration, should be named as co-authors. To all of them truly goes the credit. However, certain individuals have made specific and clear contributions to this process and will be identified as such at the appropriate times and places.

I would like to acknowledge five Brothers in particular for their impact. First is our late Brother, Nelson King, who passed before this work was published. Next is Brother Philip J. Buta, for his inspiration in assisting me in developing a broader, more comprehensive understanding of Freemasonry. Brothers Chad E. Simpson and Steven B. VanSlyck for their persistent efforts working in the quarries of Speculative Masonry, and contributing greatly to the development of the ideas that are the foundations of Arts and Sciences Lodge.

Lastly I need to thank MWB Terry W. Posey, Past Grand Master of the Grand Lodge of Ohio, serving in 2010. His first act as Grand Master was to sign the dispensation allowing Arts and Sciences to function and whose last act as Grand Master was to sign the charter of Arts and Sciences Lodge. This work is due, in part, to the admonition given me upon him presenting the dispensation for Arts and Sciences Lodge No. 792, which charged us to "go forth and multiply."

# Table of Contents

**Foreword** — v

**Author's Notes** — vii

**Introduction**
The Nature of Human Nature — 1
Fraternal Organizations — 6
Freemasonry — 10

**Part 1**
Fundamental Principles of the Craft Driven Lodge — 17
Principle 1:  Everyone Has a Voice — 20
Principle 2:  Everyone Sees The Vision — 27
Principle 3:  Everyone Has a Role — 34
Principle 4:  The Role of Leadership — 38

**Part 2**
The Arts and Sciences Experience
Introduction — 48
Chapter 1:  The Origin — 49
Chapter 2:  Early Planning — 50
Chapter 3:  Developing the Vision — 52
Chapter 4:  Learning the Ground Rules — 54
Chapter 5:  Implementing the Vision — 57
Chapter 6:  The Lodge Experience — 64
Chapter 7:  Craft Driven Decision-Making In Action — 68
Chapter 8:  The Purpose of Lodge Meetings — 73
Chapter 9:  The Agenda — 76
Chapter 10: Ritual Work — 81
Chapter 11: Candidate Education — 99
Chapter 12: Developing Lodge Leadership — 102
Chapter 13: The Lodge in the Community — 106

**Conclusion** — 109

# Appendix

**Appendix 1** — 111
The Formation of a Craft Driven Lodge
Daniel D. Hrinko

**Appendix 2** — 117
What a Lodge Can Truly Be
Steven B. Van Slyck

**Appendix 3** — 125
Statement of Principles of Arts and Sciences Lodge
Steven B. Van Slyck

**Appendix 4** — 137
Preparation
Carl Claudy

**Appendix 5** — 141
The Progressive Line in Freemasonry
Daniel D. Hrinko

**Appendix 6** — 147
From Profane to Master
Chad Simpson

**Appendix 7** — 152
On Being Master of Arts and Sciences Lodge
Daniel D. Hrinko

**Suggested Readings** — 167

# Illustrations

| | |
|---|---|
| Consecration of Arts & Sciences, photograph 2010 | 6 |
| "The West", photograph 2011 | 10 |
| "In the Beginning", photograph 2014 | 14 |
| "Working Tools", photograph 2014 | 17 |
| "Shaping the Future", photograph 2014 | 20 |
| "Charges of a Freemason", photograph 2014 | 27 |
| "Symbols of Authority", photograph 2014 | 43 |
| Arts & Sciences Logo, Graphic Image 2009 | 48 |
| "Planning and Preparation", photograph 2014 | 50 |
| "The Seven Steps", photograph 2014 | 52 |
| "Ritual and Rules", photograph 2014 | 54 |
| "Our Common Bond", photograph 2014 | 59 |
| "The Vote", photograph 2014 | 68 |
| "Instructing the Craft", photograph 2014 | 73 |
| "Following the Plan", photograph 2014 | 76 |
| "Entry to the Order", photograph 2014 | 81 |
| "Sign of Fidelity", photograph 2014 | 88 |
| "The Badge of a Mason", stained glass, Ohio Masonic Home | 93 |
| "The Middle Chamber", oil on canvas, Don Muncy, 2013 | 95 |
| "Called From Labor", graphite on paper, Peter Hrinko 2010 | 97 |

All illustrations by the Author unless otherwise noted.

# Introduction:

# The Nature of Human Nature

> "Ceremonies were instituted originally to give an external form to an internal act; but where the internal power to perform such acts does not exist, a ceremony will avail nothing and achieve nothing. You can go on making nominal Masons by the thousand, but you will only be creating a large organization of men who remain as unenlightened in the Mysteries as they always were. You cannot make a single real Initiate, save, as our teaching indicates, by the help of God and the earnest intelligent co-operation of those qualified to assist to the Light a fellow-being who, from his heart and not merely from his lips, desires that Light, humbly confessing himself spiritually poor, worthless, immersed in darkness, and unable to find that Light elsewhere or by his own efforts. For real Initiation means an expansion of consciousness from the human to the divine level."
> **- Bro. Walter Leslie Wilmshurst (1867-1929)**

Through evolution and adaptation, humans have lost many of those physical skills and qualities that allowed us to survive as isolated individuals. In place of these physical characteristics, we have developed social characteristics highlighted by interdependence. Through the use of our intellectual skills, we have learned that we are far more capable of not only surviving but thriving by relying on each other in social groups. This allows us to aggregate our various diverse skills and talents and, as a group, function more effectively than any of us can as individuals.

To maintain and further develop these interdependent relationships, evolution has provided us with emotional responses to those situations and relationships that have proven to be beneficial to our mutual existence. Through these emotions, we experience a sense of joy and comfort when participating in these relationships. Conversely, we experience sadness, fear, and desperation in such relationships that do not exist or are not contributing to our long-term survival. As a result, our emotions serve as cues to inform us about the nature of our situation, our status within relationships, and, indirectly, the impact these directions have on our long-term survival as individuals and, ultimately, as a species.

As interdependent relationships became structured, groups of humans formed systematic ways of understanding their world, characterizing these relationships, and created boundaries and expectations pertaining to these relationships that fundamentally contributed to their long-term survival. Modern man has described these ancient complex sets of relationships as tribal societies.

These societies developed structural elements that have persisted across time, culture, and geographical location. They include qualities such as the development of a system of leadership and authority, the recognition of certain individuals as having unique and individual capabilities, the production of food, the raising of children, the construction of housing, and the perpetuation of these systems of beliefs. Each of these qualities and sets of skills are organized in a manner that the entire group or tribe can benefit from each member's contribution.

These social groups or tribal societies developed rules and guidelines regarding how, when, and under what circumstances to organize and exercise these capabilities. The goal of these rules was to pursue the mutually beneficial existence that has proven to be so effective for thousands of years. Each of these societies developed a specific culture which included strategies for dealing with those who complied with the expectations of society and contributed to the needs of others through various forms of recognition and rewards. In addition, strategies were developed to deal with those who exhibited undesirable behaviors such as selfishness, laziness, or otherwise mistreated and abused those within the culture.

In each case, these timeless qualities of a culture allowed it to function and had as its foundation adherence to the fundamental concept of trustworthiness and accountability. As individuals discover their strengths, develop their talents, and take their place within the societies, they are expected to perform those duties within the guidelines of that society to make a net contribution. Without the concept of trustworthiness and accountability, societies rapidly deteriorate into chaos based upon selfishness and dishonesty.

As individuals functioning within this society, we agree to subject ourselves to the restrictions imposed by that society in return for certain benefits. These benefits often include mutual protection from others. Another is the ability to benefit from the labor of others. Just as a warrior is able to fend off enemies to protect the others in his tribe, the farmer is able to produce the food to feed not only himself but the warrior who protects him from those common enemies. Such reciprocal relationships rely upon the warrior trusting that the farmer will share his bounty, and the farmer trusting that the warrior will exercise his skills to the benefit of the farmer.

When an individual demonstrates a particularly valuable skill, they are often invested with power, authority, and influence over those around them. This allows that individual to have significant control over decisions about how the society functions, who gets benefits, rewards, and even going as far as determining mating strategies.

As humans, we find such opportunities for power and influence to be quite intoxicating. This characteristic appears to be designed to encourage us to develop greater motivation to continue positive behaviors designed to advance the overall welfare of the society and culture in which we live. However, there is a risk that the human flaw of selfishness will rear its ugly head. When behaving selfishly, opportunities for power and control will be used to benefit the individual and those in close association with the individual at the expense of the society as a whole. When this occurs, the positive desires for power, control, and adulation become destructive to the society as a whole and will likely contribute to its deterioration.

As individuals, we experience conflicting desires and drives. On one hand, we enjoy the attention, respect, and privileges that go with social approval. We may also enjoy the admiration of others based upon our ability to successfully contribute to the quality of life of those within our social group. On the other hand, we are plagued with desires to find "the easy way" and sometimes look for shortcuts to the rewards of our society without investing the efforts necessary to earn them.

As a participant in such a system, it is essential that we have an opportunity to participate in the larger decision-making process in some manner to assure that our thoughts, opinions, and ideas are considered when the decisions are made that affect the entire social group. Without a means of participating in the decision-making process that is acceptable to us, we are likely to resent making our contributions to the group, may withhold the fruits of our talents, and, indirectly, begin to lose trust in the social system as a whole. When this occurs, we begin to contribute to the decline in deterioration of that social system.

In modern society, we have developed and made use of technology to a very high level which, in many ways, masks the underlying architecture of society. However, when one looks beneath the surface, all of these key elements of what we call a tribal society remain in place. When social problems are identified, causes explored, and remedies proposed, the wise will quickly see that the foundational element of a tribal society including trust is an essential part of any successful outcome.

These universal principles of human behavior form the underlying concepts upon which the Craft Driven Lodge concepts are built. The remainder of this book will look at human nature under four key principles that are necessary elements for any organization to thrive. By following a process that recognizes the inherent need to fulfill these human characteristics and allows them to be positive forces within the development of the Lodge, the members can create a dynamic, flexible, and responsive organization that will meet their needs as individuals within the structure of the principals, allegories, symbols, and lessons of modern-day Speculative Masonry.

# The Role of Fraternal Organizations

> Freemasonry is 'veiled in allegory and illustrated by symbols' because these are the surest way by which moral and ethical truths may be taught. It is not only with the brain and with the mind that the initiate must take Freemasonry but also with the heart.
> **- Bro. Carl H. Claudy (1879-1957)**

As modern societies have developed larger and more complex social and political systems that encompassed increasingly larger groups of individuals, certain benefits have been derived. First is the benefit of an economy of scale where pooling the resources of tens of thousands of people produces the opportunity to support greater resources for security and services to the benefit of our basic security. In addition, such a large pooling of resources allows for groups of individuals to have greater influence over other groups of individuals to protect their chosen social and political structure. For example a country that has 100,000 citizens has access to far greater resources than a country with 10,000 citizens allowing the larger to impose its will on the smaller with ease.

However, a progressively larger pool of individuals can have its drawbacks. It will result in a dilution of the individual's ability to contribute to decisions and influence the behaviors of the social system. In a small tribal society, an individual may be one voice in 100 and be able to form relationships and gather informal power based upon his contribution to the welfare of the group. This allows him to have a direct influence on the decisions about the actions and activities of the group.

However, as one member in a society of 100,000, the opportunity to make a difference is greatly reduced. This contributes to a sense of powerlessness and will lead to apathy resulting in a significant reduction in an individual's willingness to participate and contribute to the welfare of the society as a whole. This forces the society to create additional rules, demands, and expectations for the individual in order to coerce the individual into continuing their contributions to the society under threat of sanctions and punishments. This is an attempt to avoid parasitic behavior which draws resources away from the larger society to the benefit of the individual without regard for the negative impact it will have on the long-term health of the society.

To counteract the feeling of being lost within a vast ocean of individuals, small subgroups develop within the societies. These subgroups often form around basic ideas, values, or shared experiences and provide an opportunity to fulfill our emotional need to be worthwhile, valued, and to make a difference. These subgroups develop their own organizational structure with the goal of reinforcing and perpetuating these values common to the members.

In the past, these subgroups have formed around common sets of experiences including skills and activities. This is likely the basis for the development of the trade guilds. As individuals developed specific skills that benefited society, these individuals who practiced the skills garnered respect and admiration for their ability to contribute to the well-being of those around them. These guilds then developed a self-perpetuating system that was designed to protect and perpetuate the trades. This process assured that the skills developed by one group of individuals are transmitted to the next generation. To maintain the respectable character they had developed within the society around them, these guilds began to include moral components to their teachings to assure that the individuals who were practicing these trades would protect the reputation of others who participated in that trade. This would assure an ongoing flow of admiration, respect, and influence in their local society fulfilling a fundamental human need necessary for the long-term success of all societies.

Fraternal societies as we know them today likely evolved from such trade guilds and other groups formed by individuals gathering around a common skill, belief, or desire. Although these societies held no formal power within the socio-political system, within their neighborhoods and immediate friends, they began to develop greater and greater influence. As with all informal groups with in a socio-political system, their influence was directly related to the manner in which they conducted themselves and to the degree in which they contributed to the general advancement and well-being of society as a whole.

Fraternal societies often contributed to the society in ways that were otherwise absent from the formal socio-political system. They offered support for those in need in the form of charitable resources, social activities, and were often a source of entertainment. For the men participating within these fraternal societies, it created opportunities to personally benefit by developing skills both professionally and socially, providing an opportunity to apply their skills to the benefit of those around them, and providing an opportunity to experience the pride and satisfaction of making a difference and seeing the efforts of their work in the lives of their community. These opportunities which were often absent in the larger socio-political system, allowed a man to feel complete, worthwhile, and able to make a difference which are essential elements to the long-term survival of the society.

As we see how a man in a fraternal society both contributes and benefits from his involvement, it becomes clear that the amount of effort a man will invest into a fraternal society is directly related to the opportunities he has within that fraternal society to develop skills, apply those skills, and make a difference in the lives of those around him. Such opportunities will draw men to these societies who are seeking a means of fulfilling our fundamental human needs. However, as these societies restrict or eliminate opportunities to develop skills, apply the skills, and, therefore, make a difference in the lives of those around them, men will then no longer become involved with such societies seeing them as a frivolous use of time with no benefit to assisting them at meeting their fundamental needs.

On a broader scale, it becomes clear that the status and influence the fraternal organization has within the society as a whole is directly related to the real and perceived benefits the organization offers to that society. As a society recognizes the value the fraternal organization offers to the advancement and betterment of that society, the level of respect, admiration, and influence will increase. This will draw the attention of men from the society to become involved in that fraternal organization. Conversely, as the contributions made by the fraternal organization to the advancement and betterment of the society as a whole declines, the respect, admiration, and influence of the organization will likewise decline.

# Freemasonry

> We represent a fraternity that believes in justice and truth and honourable action in our community . . . men who are endeavouring to be better citizens . . . to make a great country greater. This is the only institution in the world where we can meet on the level all sorts of people who want to live rightly.
> **- Bro. Harry S. Truman (1884-1972), 33rd U.S. President 1945-53, Past Grand Master Grand Lodge of Missouri.**

Speculative Masonry has been organized in its current form since 1717, with the establishment of the Grand Lodge of England, although records clearly indicate that Freemasonry, on an operative level, has been working in a Lodge or guild format for many centuries prior to that date. Masonic scholars continue to debate about when and how the transition began to occur from a purely operative craft into a speculative craft focused solely on the moral development of the individual. This debate is better suited to those more knowledgeable than I am regarding the specific documentation, hypotheses, and speculation that surround such matters.

Suffice it to say, Freemasonry, has functioned for the past 3 centuries, has been primarily a speculative art that, to some degree or another, purports to teach morality and lessons through symbols, allegories, and other experiences. Rituals have developed around the globe that include universal qualities that are typically included in the concept of "regularity." These include a belief in a single deity who is the fundamental architect or creator of all that is around us. It also includes the use of the tools of the operative stonemason as symbols to illustrate important concepts of morality and teaching moral truths. A third essential element is the tolerance of differences among men to celebrate the universal concepts that underlie a relationship which include "Brotherly love, relief, and truth."

In the modern era, after the establishment of the Grand Lodge of England in 1717, Lodges have been defined as a group of Free and Accepted Masons duly assembled with the proper furniture and a charter, warrant, or dispensation empowering them to work.

In the early days of Freemasonry, before the Grand Lodge era, it appears that Lodges functioned based upon the will of the Brothers that belonged to a particular Lodge with them participating in a decision-making process regarding leadership, rules, and modes of operation. Modern records clearly indicate that even the nature of the ritual was decided on a local level.

With the advent of the formation of Grand Lodges, standards and consistency across the Lodges were promoted. It should be noted that these overarching bodies were first formed to promote regularity among Lodges regarding those fundamental principles and to aid in the support of the health and well-being of those Lodges. In other words, the Grand Lodges were formed to serve the needs of the constituent Lodges.

During the first century of modern Speculative Masonry, Lodges were very diverse in their character in nature as they reflected the interests of the Brothers who belonged to that Lodge. Decisions continued to be made on a local level which allowed the Lodge to evolve in response to the changing interests, desires, and goals of the Brothers that belonged to that Lodge and to reflect the societal context in which the Lodge operated while continuing to adhere to those fundamental, universal principles of Freemasonry.

As Grand Lodges became more influential, they began involving themselves in attempting to control the specific activities of Lodges, to standardize the work within their jurisdictions, and to encourage greater uniformity within their jurisdictions. Superficially, this appears to make sense because it leads to the benefits of any cooling of resources which include a larger economy of scale for administrative operations, and ease of recognition between individual Lodges, and greater uniformity within the Masonic experience. These all contribute to the efficiency in the operation of Freemasonry, the organization. However, like all actions, there are often unintended consequences. Like with tribal societies, one of the difficulties with the pooling of resources was that it became more difficult for individual participants to have an impact on the nature of their Masonic experience. In addition, it made it more difficult for individual Lodges to influence decisions and to develop and retain a unique character that reflected the specific wishes and desires of the members in a particular Lodge. Just as larger political systems may have their social and economic benefits, larger Masonic organizations are often accompanied by a loss of individual opportunity, a dilution of the power of the individual, and a lack of opportunity for individual participation in the overall decision-making process.

In addition to the inevitable dilution of individual opportunity within a large system, there is the intoxicating nature of the recognition and authority associated with the rank and privileges of the Grand Lodge officers. This increases the likelihood of the abuse of their authority to insist on actions from local Lodges that serve the need of the Grand Lodge often at the expense of the local Lodge. As Grand Lodges, driven by a desire to promote the growth and development of Freemasonry, has offered many policies focused on the size and social status of the fraternity. This has resulted in unintended consequences which include compromising many of the fundamental and essential qualities of Freemasonry as it was originally formed. This has resulted in a "drifting off course" from the fundamental principles on which the fraternity was founded and which promoted its original growth and development.

Freemasonry has evolved away from its fundamental purpose of focusing on the moral development of the individual through the exploration of the symbols and lessons of the ritual and the ongoing process of "making good men better. Greater emphasis has been placed on charitable activities within the community which can place Freemasonry in a positive light within the community. However, when charity becomes the primary goal, the investment in the moral development of its members quickly fades to the background resulting in charity becoming a hollow act rather than an outward expression of the moral development of the members within the Lodge. It appears that modern Freemasonry finds itself in a state of transition. Many people question the relevance of Freemasonry, its traditions, and values to our modern society. The practices of Freemasonry have become increasingly stagnant resulting in the connection between the Lodge, the society, and the interest of the Brothers being strained.

# Back to Basics

By changing nothing, nothing changes.
– **Celestine Chua**

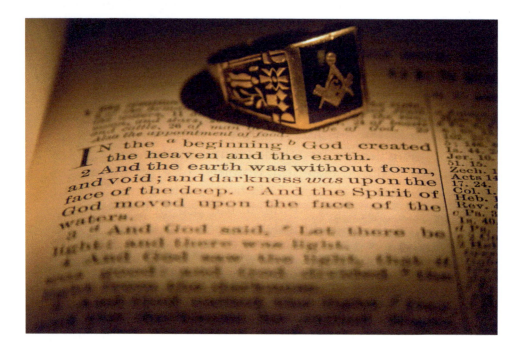

All organizations are comprised of individuals who bring with them the fundamental forces of human nature we have inherited from our ancestors. Modern businesses seek to fulfill their purpose which is to maximize profits for their investors and owners. Freemasonry, as an organization, seeks to fulfill its purpose which is to develop and maintain a system of morality through experiences and symbolism to the benefit of its members. Succeeding in this purpose will result in Freemasonry developing and maintaining relevance, influence, admiration, and respect within society. To pursue its goals, a successful modern business is constantly exploring ways of improving efficiency, effectiveness, and, therefore, profits. Although one may question the ultimate goals of modern businesses, many of the techniques developed bring forth clear, universal truths that are applicable to all organizations including Freemasonry.

For a business, the first of these is the development of a product or service that is desirable to the target audience and one of which is worth the attached price tag. In manufacturing, it is usually a tangible object like a car, mixer, or other device. In a service industry, it is an opportunity to have a task done to relieve oneself of the drudgery or to hire an expert to produce better results more efficiently. In each case, the nature of the product evolves across time as the interest and needs of the customer changes.

Looking at Freemasonry, we should ask "what is our product." Some say it is enlightenment, that Masonry offers an opportunity to explore ourselves, our purpose, and our role in society. In many ways, this view places Freemasonry in a position similar to a university.

A second way of looking at the "product" offered by Freemasonry is the opportunity to build trustworthy relationships. Through this process, we are afforded an opportunity to pledge fidelity to those around us in a fundamental commitment made by both ourselves and those around us. Through this process, we forge a bond that is symbolized by our common recognition of the hidden meanings associated with various symbols and actions. This allows us to feel confident that we are a member of "a special tribe" subject to the rules and responsibilities of this tribe while obtaining benefits comparable to our investment.

Once a business develops a product that is perceived to be of value, it must deliver the product as promised. Whenever a business fails to deliver products in a consistent, quality manner, their customers will quickly become disillusioned and no longer purchase that product or service causing the company to eventually dissolve. Therefore, the company must continue to evolve, grow, and adapt to the changing needs of the society in which they operate to assure that there is value offered to the customer.

Freemasonry is no different. If it fails to deliver the product that is promised, many of its participants will likewise fade away. There is clear evidence of the apathy of our culture expresses towards Freemasonry. The number of individuals who join is declining. There are many who join and eventually stop being involved either physically or financially. This is evidence that these members are finding that their membership is no longer worth the nominal investment of their time or finances requested.

## Part 1:

## Fundamental Principles of the Craft Driven Lodge

> New knowledge is the most valuable commodity on earth. The more truth we have to work with, the richer we become.
> **-Kurt Vonnegut**

As we look at the fundamental needs of humans as individuals and the way in which societies have been structured for thousands of years, we notice several important principles that emerge as necessary for the maintenance of a stable, working relationship between individuals and their socio-political organizations including fraternal organizations such as Freemasonry. These principles include an opportunity to influence the decision-making process, to contribute to the overall well-being of the group, to benefit from involvement in the group, and to gain a sense of pride or recognition for these efforts.

The Craft Driven Lodge recognizes several important assumptions about the nature of people. First, that everyone there is a volunteer. Second, that everyone is there for a purpose. Third, that everyone is willing to invest some effort and energy in exchange for some form of reward or benefit. Fourth that everyone has a limit to what they will tolerate before they abandon the organization.

We choose to become involved and invest our time in any activity to obtain benefits not the least of which is a chance to learn skills, apply them, and derive an emotional benefit from that sense of accomplishment that accompanies a job well done. In addition, we are driven to seek an opportunity to make a difference, influence decisions, and to obtain reasonable recognition from those around us for our efforts and contributions. We have seen these develop in the form of tribal societies, trade guilds, as well as fraternal organizations.

The Craft Driven Lodge is one where the individual members of that Lodge are in a position to direct the activities of that Lodge and to practice their desired trade, Speculative Masonry, in a manner consistent with their own needs, desires, and goals as individuals. This allows them to have a Lodge and a Masonic experience that meets their emotional needs for a sense of learning, a sense of being worthwhile, an opportunity to make a difference, and a sense of recognition for the contributions and accomplishments to the quality of life of their chosen "tribe," society, or even the life of those within the Lodge.

If you view the Lodge as a tribe, then we can begin to see how these essential elements come into play. First, there must be an underlying trust that investing in this Lodge will somehow result in a benefit to the individual. As individuals join the tribe (the Lodge) they should be encouraged to display and develop their talents to the benefit of others. Just as the farmer grows food for the warrior who protects them, the accountant should be willing to spend time as the treasurer of the Lodge to the benefit of his Brothers. Just as the warrior should be willing to go to battle to protect the farmer who provides his food, the orator with an excellent voice and good memory should assume an active role in the leadership and ritualistic work for the betterment of the Lodge.

The process of forming and operating a Craft Driven Lodge requires a thorough understanding of four important principles that drive all actions and all decisions throughout the life of this Lodge at all times.

**Principle 1: Everyone Has a Voice**
**Principle 2: Everyone Sees the Vision**
**Principle 3: Everyone Has a Role**
**Principle 4: The Leadership Lets the Workers Work**

The following sections provide a detailed explanation of each of these concepts which allows a group to organize themselves in such a manner as to provide the best opportunities for the individuals within that group to meet their needs as individuals as well as contribute to the health and well-being of the group.

# Principle 1: Everyone Has a Voice

Discussion is an exchange of knowledge; argument an exchange of ignorance.
- **(Verni) Robert Quillen (1887-1948)**

We can forgive a child who is afraid of the dark; the real tragedy of life is when men are afraid of the light.
– **Plato**

For an individual functioning within an organization it is essential that there be a clear way for an individual's thoughts, observations, desires, and opinions to be heard regarding decisions, directions, and the operations of any organization. Tribal societies have long established guidelines for a process where every member has an opportunity to be heard and, therefore, have influence on the decision-making process within the limits of their status within the society and their contributions to that society.

When we recognize that every man who comes to Masonry is seeking something, it is incumbent upon the Lodge to do whatever we can to learn what that something might be. It is likely that this individual is unaware of the exact nature of what is being sought and, therefore, cannot articulate it clearly. This can create a barrier and many awkward situations where Brothers may choose to say little or nothing because they lack confidence in their own ability to say something in a manner that makes sense. It is incumbent on the Lodge to designate those with better skills to assist those with weaker skills by setting an example, asking questions to assist the Brother in drawing out and articulating his thoughts and opinions, and creating opportunities for these skills to be learned and practiced in smaller settings. Like any skill, the art of discussion, the science of rhetoric, and the confidence to use new skills are well within the capability of everyone. Within a Craft Driven Lodge, it is critical that such forums be created where every member has a voice with the potential of influencing every aspect of Lodge functioning. The first step is to create an atmosphere where the Brethren are free to discuss their thoughts, ideas, and desires about what a Masonic experience could be like. This involves creating a forum where every Brother is encouraged to have a voice, express an opinion, and to share ideas based upon his knowledge, goals, and desires. This is consistent with the corporate idea of being able to "brainstorm" when reviewing the current status of a company and the direction in which it should be heading.

In many Lodges, Brothers defer to the Master of that Lodge due to the formal structure. It is very autocratic and authoritarian. In some ways, the Master of a Lodge could be referred to as a benevolent dictator. Although such a formal structure may be symbolically important, such a literal interpretation can result in a system whereby the Master imposes his will on the Lodge during his year(s) of service in an attempt to draw attention to himself without regard for the impact it may have on the long-term health of the Lodge or even the interests and desires of those in the Lodge.

A careful reading of many installation ceremonies will indicate that the Master is expected to make decisions and to rule with the best interest of the Lodge in mind avoiding those human frailties such as selfishness, favoring one group over another, or reveling in the limelight. However, these installation ceremonies say very little about understanding how meeting the needs of the members, who are your workforce, will have a dramatic impact on your ability to accomplish anything during "your year in the East." It is important to remember that the master serves "at the will and pleasure of the Lodge."

Therefore, the wise Master will go to great lengths to learn what the members of the Lodge wish to see happen within their Lodge and find ways to attend to those desires and needs as he organizes the work of the Lodge for the time he serves. In addition, the members of that Lodge should make use of opportunities to express themselves regarding their thoughts and opinions about the Lodge and its activities.

> In all affairs it's a healthy thing now and then to hang a question mark on the things you have long taken for granted.
> **– Bertrand Russell**

In the Craft Driven Lodge, the regular use of planning meetings and open discussions during these sessions are an essential element to providing a formal opportunity for any member interested in the activities of the Lodge to have an active voice in the decisions being made about the life of the Lodge. The Worshipful Master of a Craft Driven Lodge is expected to organize, promote, and encourage open participation in these planning meetings where he, like any good CEO, is surveying his "customers" regarding what they want from the organization as well as determining what investments they are ready to make in the success of this organization. Thinking of the membership as "customers" is to realize that these men have paid their money, experienced the rituals, and are investing their time. They do this in the expectation that Masonic activities will yield benefits not the least of which are opportunities to learn and apply skills, make a difference in the lives of themselves and those around them, and to obtain reasonable recognition for these successes.

These discussions should have a focus about a particular topic, aspect of Lodge operation, or other narrowly defined area of concern. It is helpful to these discussions to bring in additional information from various sources to help expand the realm of possibilities available to the Brothers. Bringing in published materials from Masonic scholars, philosophers, authors of the past, or even speakers from other Lodges can provide new information about the possible practices of Speculative Masonry to expand the menu of choices available.

When forming a new Lodge or beginning to consider the evolution of an existing Lodge in a direction more desirable for the membership, discussions should include numerous topics including the overall goal of a Masonic meeting as well as specific topics such as how certain tasks are accomplished. These questions can be used during the discussions to help the Brothers begin to identify what they would like to have their Lodge experience be.

> Failure is not fatal, but failure to change might be.
> **– John Wooden**

Questions that can be used to start beneficial discussions:
- *What would a perfect Lodge meeting look like?*
- *What could happen before the Lodge opens that would contribute to a sense of Brotherhood and preparation for the meeting to be conducted?*

- *How could the opening ceremony contribute to the Lodge experience?*

- *How could the minutes be handled?*

- *How could the bills be handled?*

- *How could visitors be welcomed into the Lodge?*

- *How could decisions be made regarding social activities, charitable activities, and upcoming events of the Lodge?*

- *How could the educational components be presented at the meeting?*

- *How could new Brothers be welcomed into the Lodge?*

- *How could Entered Apprentices and fellow crafts be welcomed into the Lodge?*

- *How could introductions be handled?*

- *How long should a meeting last?*

- *What would happen on a night when ritual was being presented?*

- *What could happen after the closing of the Lodge to add to the fraternal experience?*

- *What would you like to see in our Lodge during the next meeting, the upcoming year, in future years?*

As the Brothers discuss the topics noted above and decisions are made, they should be documented in some manner to assure that decisions are not being reinvented at every meeting and that some form of consistency evolves.

It is essential to recognize that the process of holding numerous discussions involving interested Brothers is likely to occur over a period of months if not years to assure that each of these topics is adequately and thoroughly addressed. It is important to note that, as the process moves forward, a consensus will likely form about what the Lodge should be doing, the way it should be going about its work, and the kind of experience the Brothers involved would like to have.

During the discussions, you may learn that some individuals are adamantly attached to certain elements of what they believe should be part of Freemasonry and, if the group does not adhere to that concept, that the individual may no longer wish to participate in that particular Lodge activity. This should not be considered a failure but requires the recognition that not everybody is interested in the same kind of Lodge experience. Just as we have many different kinds of cars to get us from point A to point B, we should encourage the development of various kinds of Lodges. This will allow those with differing interests, focuses, and desires to have a Masonic experience tailored to their desires with all Lodge experiences being based on those same universal and fundamental principles of what constitutes Speculative Masonry.

Including individual Brothers in the discussions regarding the most basic of decisions, even the most minor details, will have four critical benefits that will eventually support the long-term success of the Lodge. First, it puts that individual Brother in a position to feel valued, respected, and able to contribute in whatever manner they can. Second, by participating in this process, they invest "sweat equity" in the health and well-being of the organization. Third, it builds a strong personal connection between that Brother and that Lodge resulting in a sense of pride that will reward the Brother participating in the Lodge as the Lodge succeeds. Fourth, it builds a strong connection between the Brothers as they establish a common goal and labor together in the quarries to bring their goals to fruition.

As new Brothers are Initiated, Passed, and Raised in this Lodge, they too should be included in the discussions, decision-making, and provided an opportunity to believe that they are personally responsible for the long-term health and success of this Lodge and that by building this relationship, they too will share in the responsibility and invest accordingly.

## Principle 2 - Everyone Sees the Vision

In the absence of clearly-defined goals, we become strangely loyal to performing daily trivia until ultimately we become enslaved by it.
– **Robert Heinlein**

If the greatest enemy of action is the lack of a plan, the greatest enemy of a plan is the lack of action.
– **Laura Stack**

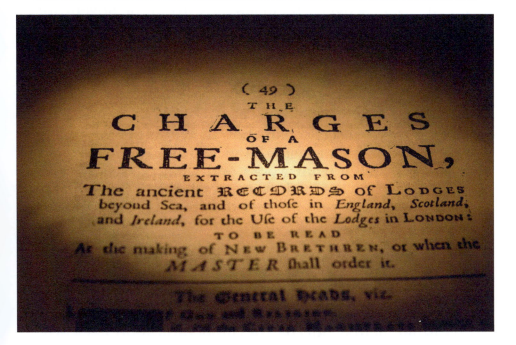

In Freemasonry we speak at length about the importance of the Trestle Board. The Trestle Board is the place where the architect lays down his designs. This requires great thought and the ability to see "the big picture" whereby the purpose of the building, the necessary space, design, and structures necessary are all considered before the first stone meets stone. This careful thought and understanding about how one part fits with the other and influences the eventual outcome is an essential element to all successful endeavors including the creation and operation of a Craft Driven Lodge.

Imagine being invited to go on a trip. You are not told how long the trip will be, not told how you will be traveling, where you will be going, nor the route which you will follow. You were simply told to sign up, trust us, and go along for the ride. This is a situation that will lead to many questions and high levels of uncertainty. It may even lead to being uncomfortable to the point of abandoning the trip at the first opportunity to return home to a place of known comfort and security. It definitely is not the kind of situation that would lead to an eager passenger who looks forward to the adventure that may lie ahead.

In joining a Lodge, we ask our new Brother, ritualistically, to place themselves in that very situation. The activities we can pursue which will reduce this uncomfortability are to gain a clear vision about what this Lodge is attempting to accomplish, how it will be going about accomplishing that vision, and learning from the past both in terms of what works and what does not work. When we plan a social event, we need to understand how that social event fits into the greater picture of how this Lodge operates. When we work with candidates, we need to know how the candidate education fits into the greater picture of how this Lodge operates.

Corporations and organizations have long understood the value of *"a mission statement"* or *"a vision"* whereby the fundamental purpose of the organization is clearly articulated and serves as that Master blueprint upon which everything else is built. Lodges, like corporations and other successful organizations, should also have a clearly defined mission or "vision" whereby every member is able to understand the ultimate goal toward which they are working and see how their role as a part of bringing this idea to fruition.

When reflecting on our Masonic lessons, two particular documents come to mind. First, nearly every charter I have ever seen specifically states that the purpose of the Lodge is to "make Masons." This statement tells me that a primary purpose of the Lodge is to not only be administratively sound and conduct the ritual work, but go to great lengths to assist a man in that process of transformation from the profane to the truly skilled speculative Mason.

The second document that stands out in my mind is our ritual when, in the Entered Apprentice degree, a simple question teaches us the importance of learning, subduing our passions, and improving ourselves as Masons. It, therefore, is a responsibility of any Lodge to provide opportunities for this learning to occur as a brother's skills in Speculative Masonry develop.

It is also important for any Lodge to develop a vision specific to them and their goals of operation within this greater umbrella of Speculative Masonry. This vision should include a clear understanding as to the specific goals of that particular Lodge and the way they practice Freemasonry to assure that the fundamental needs of the members are being met whereby there are opportunities to develop skills, apply those skills, and to reap the benefits both in terms of satisfaction and recognition for their successful efforts.

In the first principle of assuring that everyone has a voice, the use of planning meetings was highly recommended as the first critical step in following the process necessary to have a Craft Driven Lodge. Numerous topics were suggested, many of which involve specific details about the Masonic experience. However, during the early phases of a Lodge's development, no topic should be considered "out of bounds." This will avoid the Brothers being limited by the "traditions" of an existing Lodge or of the local customs of that region. Discussions could involve exploring what it means to be a Mason, what the purpose of a Lodge is, and various ways of operating based upon all the options available. This process should be geared towards developing a clear understanding of the "vision" of the Lodge and a consensus about what constitutes "the perfect Lodge meeting, the meeting you wouldn't want to miss."

This process is similar to sitting down with a map when planning a vacation and holding a discussion with everyone going on the trip to determine a destination. Without a clear destination, it is impossible to plot a reasonable and appropriate route. Without a reasonable and appropriate route to guide your every step, it is impossible to know if you are straying from that path upon which you have set yourself. Without having a clear destination and route to follow, we will experience aimless wandering in the wilderness. We will take many actions and make many decisions that are counterproductive, with many unintended consequences to the detriment of the organization, and contribute to the failure of that organization.

These concepts can be applied in two different scenarios; one being the formation of a new Lodge. The other is an existing Lodge exploring ways to develop and fulfill its potential. These two different paths will be explored separately.

## Formation of a New Lodge

> We must become the change we want to see.
> **– Mahatma Gandhi**

When Brothers meet to form a new Lodge, they are faced with several opportunities and numerous barriers. The best way to describe the opportunities is that we are presented with a clean sheet of paper and given the chance to design a Lodge and its related Masonic experience without the hindrance or barriers of "traditions" or ingrained past practices. There is no grouping of Past Masters sitting on the sideline grumbling "we never did it that way when I was Master." We are free from the albatross of "we've never done it that way" and its cousin "we've always done it this way." Such an opportunity is rare but can set the stage for splendid and unexpected results.

The challenges these Brothers face is that decisions must be made about how every single thing will be done down to the smallest detail. You have no pattern of established practices, many of which are beneficial, from which to draw to expedite the operation of this Lodge by adopting or continuing many of these practices. Therefore, the formation process will likely be longer and far more tedious than might seem expected at first.

Another challenge is that new Lodges are typically formed by Brothers from several existing Lodges and bring with them their own opinions and preferences about what constitutes good Masonic work at all levels and in all ways. This can lead to some lively but lengthy discussions about anything and everything which further contributes to the time necessary for a Lodge to truly form and develop its own identity as compromises are reached, discussions held, and even hurt feelings salved.

## The Evolution of an Existing Lodge

> Things never were "the way they used to be."
> Things never will be "the way it's going to be someday."
> Things are always just the way they are for the time being.
> And the time being is always in motion.
> **– A. E. Xenopouloudakis**

When a group of Brothers within a particular Lodge begin to meet and discuss their thoughts and opinions about the operation of their Lodge, they are initiating a process that can result in wonderful outcomes. It is impossible to imagine that every member is perfectly satisfied with their Lodge exactly the way it is. It is important to the long-term health and well-being of each Lodge to periodically discuss the activities of the Lodge, the way it operates, and the way it approaches the practice of Speculative Masonry.

These discussions will create opportunities for Brothers to help the Lodge evolve and remain relevant to its membership in particular and society as a whole. It can also assist the Lodge in remaining firmly connected to the fundamental principles of Freemasonry. These discussions are likely to generate ideas about how things can be done in a manner that is somewhat different than "the way it's always been" for many years.

As this process begins, differences of opinion are likely to arise. To assist in this process, it is important that these discussions include as many members of the Lodge as is possible, taking special care to include those who are vocal about various points of view. To maintain harmony within these discussions, it is wise to identify a respected individual to act as a facilitator or "traffic cop" to keep the discussion focused on ideas rather than allowing it to degenerate into personal discussions.

These discussions should be held in a manner that is respectful of the traditions of the Lodge, but raise questions about the purpose and utility of everything that is done. If a practice that has been part of the Lodge's life for many years still holds value and purpose, then it makes sense to keep that practice as long as the purpose is understood and the value perceived by all. However, if a practice is included in the life of the Lodge for reasons that are unknown to the participants, then it will be done in a bland, lifeless manner and will take on the trappings of a bad habit rather than as an opportunity to contribute to the Masonic experience.

As the discussions continue, an existing Lodge should identify 1-3 particular changes that seem to be most closely connected with the idea of bringing vitality to the Lodge in a manner consistent with the goals of that Lodge. For example, if that Lodge prides itself on its community and charitable involvement, then exploring different ways of bringing more attention, vitality, and greater involvement in those activities could be one of the first areas to be explored. If that Lodge is concerned about the quality of the ritual work, then different ways to explore how the ritual was delivered, the way ritualists are trained, and the opportunities for involvement by greater numbers of Brothers in the ritual can be considered as a way of bringing life and vitality to the Lodge. If that Lodge is concerned with exploring the deeper meanings and applications of Masonic symbolisms and the lessons within the ritual, then opportunities to read, share, and explore these matters should be a focus of activities both within the Lodge meeting and outside of the Lodge meeting.

By considering all the possibilities and exploring different ways of practicing Speculative Masonry, then the Lodge will remain aware of and responsive to the members who are active in that Lodge meeting their needs and desires and keeping them active and involved in their Lodge.

In general, as Lodges began to discuss the nature of their practices of Speculative Masonry, they should be focusing on clarifying and communicating to the members a clear idea of what the Lodge and Lodge experience should be. Since everyone involved with a Craft Driven Lodge has an opportunity to participate in these discussions and contribute to the eventual collection of ideas, they will be able to meet several fundamental human needs. Most importantly, that ability to make a difference and to have influence and input into the decisions of their "tribe," or Lodge, will be made available to them. As the Brothers understand what the common goal is, then they will be prepared to put their shoulder to the wheel to bring this dream to fruition which will be discussed at length in the next section.

# Principle 3 - Everyone Has a Role

> Vision without execution is hallucination.
> **– Thomas A. Edison**
>
> The way to get started is to stop talking and begin doing.
> **– Walt Disney**
>
> Stop the mindless wishing that things would be different. Rather than wasting time and emotional and spiritual energy in explaining why we don't have what we want, we can start to pursue other ways to get it.
> **– Greg Anderson**
>
> It is not by the intellectual attainment of oral expression that we become Masons, but by the way in which we acquire the science and couple it with the art of temple building, and practice it in our everyday association with our fellow men. No degree of Masonry is of any avail, unless it bears fruit in action.
> **– Bro. Gerald Ford, 38th President of the United States**

In modern organizations, one of the greatest challenges being faced is a lack of understanding by the worker of how he contributes to and benefits from the overall success of the organization. When this understanding fails to be developed, then specific directions are questioned, often ignored, and are treated as autocratic orders rather than actions that will benefit everyone. This contributes to the sense of powerlessness, worthlessness, and apathy that prevents someone from actively contributing the talents they have to that organization.

However, when an organization makes it clear that everyone involved is directly connected and part of the success of the organization, then numerous problems fade from the landscape and many positive goals of both the individual and the organization are achieved.

In the Masonic fraternity, we become involved to participate in an interactive relationship between ourselves and the organization. We expect the organization to offer a structured way in which we can learn, participate, develop as individuals, and apply what we have learned to the benefit of those around us. In exchange for this, we look forward to reasonable and appropriate recognition. These opportunities fulfill a fundamental human need and can be seen as a worthwhile use of our time if those needs are fulfilled.

In a Lodge with identified positions of officers, there are a limited number of places within any Lodge for an individual to serve in a formal capacity. We need but one Master, two Wardens, two Deacons, two Stewards, a Treasurer, a Secretary, and a Tyler. In some jurisdictions, other formal positions may exist providing additional opportunities to contribute to the life and success of the Lodge. However, it is important that those who do not hold formal positions be afforded an opportunity to contribute to the health and well-being of the Lodge. These opportunities should recognize individuals with certain skills and capabilities and allow them to demonstrate their talents to the Brothers.

The man who can cook should be afforded an opportunity to demonstrate his skills to the Lodge. A man with a flexible schedule can be afforded an opportunity to arrive earlier than others to help prepare the Lodge for the meeting. The Brother with social contacts and organizational skills may serve on a committee for the activities of the Lodge within the community. The Brother with a good story, firm handshake, and welcoming voice can be the person identified to assure that all visitors are attended to, and made to feel welcome.

Those with the facility to learn ritual should be afforded an opportunity to participate in the ritual activities of the Lodge even if they do not hold a formal position or desire to assume a formal role of leadership. Those with a propensity for understanding the concepts of teaching can be afforded an opportunity to work with new Brothers in various ways to assist them in learning the lessons of Freemasonry through formal and informal instruction.

Brothers may enter the Lodge with few known or developed skills. However, all have the potential for the development of skills that have yet to be recognized. As Freemasonry promotes the concept of helping "good men become better," this includes assisting a Brother who is working alongside others in the Lodge to explore and develop his talents. This affords each Brother an opportunity to be active in the life of a Lodge, make a contribution to the life and success of the Lodge, and feel that they are, in part, responsible for the overall success of everyone which is a personally satisfying and rewarding experience.

In many Lodges today, we learned that to be an active member, you must first become an officer and learn to do everything regardless of your talents or willingness to serve. This leads to individuals who have valuable skills in many areas being forced into tasks for which they are unprepared, unskilled, and ineffective. Otherwise, we become a spectator on the sidelines with no way to contribute to the life and vitality of the Lodge. This is the complete opposite of what we look for in a Masonic experience which is the chance to contribute, be successful, and gain recognition for our successes.

In a Craft Driven Lodge, we have already gone to great lengths to create an opportunity for everyone to take an active role in the discussions that underlie all decisions being made by the Lodge. We have focused our attention not only on the details of day-to-day activities, social events, and even the manner in which our ritual is performed but also on the ultimate purpose and goals of our Masonic experiences. Now comes the time to take actions to put these ideas, plans, and agreements to work as we pursue those goals set forth in the vision we have created and posted on our Lodge's trestle board.

Recognizing that everyone brings talents to the Lodge, it is important that those selected to lead the Lodge should attend to finding a place in the life of the Lodge for every single member. If everyone has a job and clearly understands how that job contributes to the life and success of the Masonic experience they have chosen to create for themselves, then they will be committed, active members. Making use of committees, sharing the responsibilities of various parts of the ritual, allowing men to "pro tem" positions as they develop their ritual skills, making use of teams of men to assist candidates in learning their required materials, and numerous other opportunities exist to provide everyone in the Lodge a chance to take on the responsibility and actively contribute to the life of the Lodge.

Not everyone is capable of mastering every job. Some are excellent speakers, others are excellent workers. It is important that no man be placed in a position where he is "set up to fail" by being "required" either by rule or by custom to perform certain tasks as an expectation of being "active" in the Lodge. Recognizing the limitations we all have and allowing us to contribute while working around those limitations will continue to make the Lodge experience a place where each of us can fulfill our fundamental human needs of being valued, making a difference, and contributing to the success and well-being of those around us.

# Principle 4 - The Role of Leadership:

# The Leadership Lets the Workers Work

> The best leader is the one who has sense enough to pick good men to do what he wants done, and self-restraint enough to keep from meddling with them while they do it.
> **- Bro. Theodore Roosevelt, 26th President of United States**

As the discussions regarding the formation of a Lodge or the ongoing development of the Lodge occur, certain individuals within the group will begin to emerge as leaders of this group. There are various styles of leadership some of which can be very beneficial to this overall process and others can be very destructive.

A review of ancient sociopolitical organizations and societies shows that there is a trade-off between efficiency and the representative nature of the decision-making process. In the sense of political models, a dictatorship is the fastest, most efficient way of making decisions and implementing them to obtain an effect. On the other end of the continuum is a pure democracy where everyone participates in every decision leading to a process that can be slow, sometimes ponderous, but sensitive to the desires of those being governed.

The same principles apply within organizations and "tribes" such as Masonic Lodges. There are those who may be articulate, insightful, but desirous of obtaining glory and recognition for themselves. They are likely to advocate a "father knows best" model and be willing to "dictate" to the rest of the Lodge what should or should not be done. Like all models of organization, this can be very efficient with decisions being made rapidly and implemented without hesitation. However, it can have a negative effect on the overall life and well-being of the organization as it is contrary to the first fundamental principle of a Craft Driven Lodge which is that everyone should have a voice or input into the decision-making process.

Freemasonry, by virtue of its structure, titles, and symbolic power is particularly prone to individuals becoming overly authoritarian in that we are told that as Worshipful Master or Grand Master of the Grand Lodge you have powers that, symbolically, are unchecked and unquestioned. Unfortunately, when people take these to heart and exercise of them from a paternal point of view, it can lead to developing a belief that the individual member has no authority or input into the decision making process.

If we recall our review of tribal societies, you will remember that individuals who feel disenfranchised or lack any form of power or control will lose confidence in the organization and stop investing in the health of the organization. This is because they no longer feel they will receive any compensation or benefit for their investment. The farmer will stop planting crops to feed the warrior if he no longer feels the warrior is concerned about the farmer's well-being.

When developing a Craft Driven Lodge, it is important to understand that, in corporate terms, the members of the Lodge served two important roles. On the surface, it is clear that they are the labor force which is a necessary element of successfully implementing any decision made or taking any actions on behalf of the Lodge. Therefore, the Worshipful Master who has no Craft willing to follow or support him is completely ineffective. Within the Craft Driven Lodge, a second role is adopted by the membership which, in corporate terms, would mean that they serve as the Board of Directors providing direction to the management team (Worshipful Master and officers of the Lodge) about what direction they would like to see the Lodge take and the activities that they are willing to support.

Therefore, those chosen to be in leadership positions, particularly the Worshipful Master, should be skilled at soliciting input from the membership about the direction, goals, and activities that will support the Masonic experience the members want. Once the discussions have yielded a clear direction for the Lodge, activities to pursue, and the talent available to make these ideas come to fruition, they should be willing to organize the labor force (the Brethren of the Lodge) and other necessary resources to implement those goals and desires. Thus, the idea of a servant/leader must involve mastering that balancing act between efficiency through directive actions and being responsive to the needs of the members.

In the concepts of servant leadership, it is important that those who have been selected to organize and implement the desires of the Lodge should refrain from overextending their power to the point of interfering in the decision-making process. As leaders become overly controlling and make unilateral decisions at an increasing rate, the membership is robbed of possibility of men stepping up in volunteering for various roles instead resulting in them waiting patiently to be appointed. Unilateral decisions are based upon the vision of the man making the unilateral decision rather than the vision of the group as a whole. This vision is likely to be hidden from the eyes of the membership and not understood. It is as if we are again pushed to the back seat of the car on that mystery trip to nowhere in particular and having a blindfold and a gag installed.

As plans are implemented, responsibilities delegated, and authority for implementation is spread among the membership, the Master and others in servant-leadership positions should trust but verify that tasks are completed. Failing to allow Brothers to succeed based upon their own merits will rob them of the opportunity of fulfilling one of our fundamental human desires: that of feeling that they make a difference and contribute to those around us. However, failing to monitor the success of those with delegated responsibilities may result in unfulfilled plans and commitments contributing to unsuccessful events. This highlights the importance of carefully assigning responsibilities to those who have the skills, time, and resources to bring each task to fruition.

When communicating with those around us, the use of language can be very powerful when it comes to expressing these ideas. For example, a particular Masonic year for the man sitting in the East is often referred to as "my year as Master" or "my year in the East." This terminology implies that the man elected and installed the sit in the East is in effect in charge and authorized to implement what he thinks is best for his Lodge. This places his ideas, his thoughts, and his desires in the primary position and encourages him to do things that, although they may be good for the Lodge, are primarily designed for him to "leave his mark" and establish a legacy as proof that he sat in that chair. This can easily become an example of the intoxicating nature of power. It will likely lead to new ideas coming every year with one Master and going out the next year when the next Master brings in his ideas leaving no room for the ideas of the Brothers and no sense of continuity across time.

However, we are free to use alternative language to refer to this situation such as "the Lodge's year" during which a man who serves as Master recognizes the fundamental concepts that he is a temporary custodian of that position and that his primary responsibility is to ascertain and implement the will of the Craft during his time in that position. He must realize that any legacy that may result from his time serving the Lodge as Worshipful Master is secondary to unimportant when compared to his ability to serve the will of the Craft during that particular year.

Should any member have any ideas about ways to improve the nature of the Masonic experience, he has always had the opportunity, as a member of that Lodge, to initiate a discussion among the members to consider a particular idea and, if adopted, participate in its implementation. By having regular planning meetings, such discussions are never more than a few weeks away and can afford clear opportunities for the first principle to be implemented, that of every member having a voice.

This appears to be in stark contrast to the way many Lodges typically operate in the 20th century. It is all too common for the members to sit passively on the sidelines waiting to see what the Master will do. Any ideas they may have are kept to themselves or, if expressed, summarily rejected for one of several reasons. One reason often heard is "we've never done it that way before" without considering the potential merits of the idea. Second, it is rejected because it is "the Masters' year" to run the Lodge and we should "do what the Master says." Third, we often hear that "if you think you can do a better job, work your way through the line and when you get to be Master, then you can do this."

These responses to ideas and suggestions take a terrible toll on the long-term health and well-being of Lodges for numerous reasons. First, it inhibits the ability of the Lodge to evolve as its membership evolves. Ways of thinking, functioning, and providing a Masonic experience become frozen at some point in time and that, although the membership changes across time and the interests of those members change as well, the way the Lodge operates does not. This results in the membership feeling that activities that once had meaning become empty, meaningless activities. It also prevents the Lodge from reacting to changes in society causing members to feel that the fraternity is irrelevant and, therefore, of no benefit to anyone.

Through discussions that solicit and reflect the interests of the membership, the members are enabled to remain in contact with the fundamental reasons why activities are pursued preventing them from becoming meaningless, empty gestures. In addition, they are free to allow the activities of the Lodge to evolve as the membership, the interest of the members, and the role of the Lodge in society changes across time. This prevents Lodges from becoming stagnant and, therefore, irrelevant.

# The Role of Grand Lodges

> We must always change, renew, rejuvenate ourselves; otherwise we harden.
> **– Johann Wolfgang von Goethe**

So far we have discussed how leadership at the Lodge level can promote or inhibit activities that can directly affect the health and well-being of the Lodge. However, with the formation of the Grand Lodge system to regulate Lodges and afford standards regarding recognition and operation, there have developed many opportunities for the misuse of position, authority, and rulemaking to further have a negative impact on the health and well-being of individual Lodges.

For any Lodge to exist with any recognition as being a "regular" Lodge, it must be chartered under a Grand Lodge that has recognition with the majority of the Grand Lodges that share similar standards of regularity.

Lodges identified as "regular" are commonly the Lodges recognized by the United Grand Lodge of England.

Grand Lodges and their constituent Lodges have developed traditions and standardized ways of operating that connect them with those who came before us as well as with others around the globe that share similar values.

If one looks at the role of a Grand Lodge from the metaphor of a sports activity, you can begin to understand how the way a Grand Lodge interacts with its constituent Lodges may either support and promote the ongoing health and well-being of the fraternity or serve to stifle it and promote stagnation.

Let us presume that we are facing an open grassy field with no lines marks or other ways of delineating it in any way. A group of men cast their eyes upon this field and decide "let's create a game called football (soccer for you American types)." For them to create this game, they need to delineate the scope of the playing field, mark those lines identifying what is "inbounds" and what is "out of bounds" and set forth basic rules for fair play. They then identify individuals who are knowledgeable about the rules to serve as referees to identify violations and react accordingly.

Rest assured that beyond the observation of the game and enforcement of the basic rules, the players are free to play within the bounds of the field. The sanctioning body (Grand Lodge) does not shape the way the game is played, the nature of the players uniforms, the strategies that may be employed, or provide specific regulations regarding the activities and responsibilities of the general players. This leaves players and coaches free to explore all the possibilities that exist within the boundaries set forth by the playing field and the basic rules of fair play.

Should the regulating body fail to provide adequate rules to clarify questions, rampant cheating and a sense of unfairness would begin to dominate the game due to a lack of structure. In such a situation, periodic reviews of the rules and adjustments should be made to assure that the spirit of fair play be maintained while keeping regulations to a practical minimum.

However, should the regulating body become overzealous in its regulations and begin to specify in great detail exactly what will be done at each point during the game, the actions of each individual player at every step of the way, and specifying what will happen next, the nature of the game will change dramatically. Those qualities that would attract someone to play the game would be lost and, after walking through the prescribed directions on several occasions, interest would be lost as would participation.

Grand Lodges, like any regulatory body, should enforce the rules regarding the "field of play" and the concept of fairness while promoting and encouraging exciting play within those rules to create a rewarding experience for all involved. A Grand Lodge has a responsibility to balance opposing forces. On one hand, there is the comfort of certainty and stability of well-considered regulations with its structuring effects, and on the other hand, the opportunity to engage in activities that are individualized to the Brothers in the Lodges allowing them to remain relevant to current society and evolve to meet the needs of the men in attendance. Too many rules and the Lodges become dull, boring, and unfulfilling. Too few rules and the Lodges become disjointed, inconsistent, and unable to maintain administrative stability.

Brothers who are members of existing Lodges and wish to explore the options available to them regarding the practice of Freemasonry in their jurisdiction should assure that they are thoroughly conversant with the expectations and regulations associated with the operation and administration of Lodges, as well as any requirements or prohibitions regarding the way ritual is performed as specified by their grand Lodge. As discussions occur regarding the options available to local Lodges when it comes to the practice of Speculative Masonry, it is important that the Grand Lodge representative appointed to work with the Brethren be kept informed about desires and that questions the clarified before actions are taken that might result in a violation of Grand Lodge rules. Regulations in some jurisdictions may be very specific about what occurs between the opening and closing of a stated communication. However, activities before a meeting, after a meeting, or while at refreshment may provide significant latitude in the practice of Speculative Masonry.

As Brothers meet with the intention of forming a new Lodge, they should be cognizant of the regulations put forth by the Grand Lodge from which they wish to obtain a dispensation or charter regarding the formation of new Lodges. Care should be taken to ensure that meetings, discussions of ritual, permissions from neighboring Lodges, and other requirements are followed to avoid creating dissent within the jurisdiction or region. It is wise to include local or regional Grand Lodge officials in the conversations regarding your desires and ask for and direction in pursuing your goal of creating a Lodge that will meet your needs.

When a Grand Lodge officer or representative is approached by a group of Brothers wishing to explore the possibilities regarding the practice of Speculative Masonry either through the evolution of an existing Lodge or the creation of a new Lodge, they should fulfill their duties to ensure the rules are being followed, but recognize that to do so in an authoritarian manner when asked for advice would be counterproductive. In addition, they should be conversant with the difference between rules and traditions one of which is required, the other being habitual. The goal of that Grand Lodge officer should be to form a collaborative relationship with these Brothers to understand their desires, goals, and aspirations. He should work with them to promote their ability to achieve those goals within the fundamental rules of the Grand Lodge.

# Part 2:

# The Arts & Sciences Experience

# Introduction

This section will chronicle the formation and evolution of Arts & Sciences Lodge No. 792 chartered by the Grand Lodge of Ohio on October 16, 2010. This section will show the implementation of the general ideas and concepts discussed in Part 1 in detail to demonstrate how these concepts were put into play in the formation of this Craft Driven Lodge.

It should be noted that many of the decisions made and activities put in place by the Brothers of Arts & Sciences Lodge were done so based upon the results of the discussions held to meet the needs of these Brothers. They are by no means presented as a blueprint for others to follow without thorough discussion and consideration of their own needs, their own interests, and their own desires. Brothers in other Lodges are free to pick and choose from any of these and implement them as they see fit to meet their own needs.

# Chapter 1 - The Origin

Arts & Sciences Lodge evolved from an informal gathering of Brothers in the central Ohio area that was called the Goose and Gridiron Social Club drawing its name from the famous tavern where the Grand Lodge of England was first formed in 1717. Two articles were published about this Lodge, in the Philalethes magazine in 2010. The first being by Brother Daniel D Hrinko; the second by Brother Steven B. VanSlyck. They can be found in the appendix.

As these articles reflect, significant effort went into the early days of forming this Lodge focusing on the ability to include everyone in the discussions and decisions regarding the nature of this Lodge, its focus, its activities, and every detail of its operation. It is also important to note that not one decision was made unilaterally by anyone. The time, effort, and "sweat equity" was invested by all involved which ensures that a strong fraternal bond is built between the Brothers as well as among the Brothers who all have a vested interest in the success of this enterprise.

## Chapter 2 - Early Planning

From early in its life as the Goose and Gridiron Social Club, it became clear that the promotion of education and a deeper understanding of Speculative Masonry was a common desire among these Brothers. Discussions often included a wide range of topics common to Freemasonry as well as other observations about various aspects of Masonic experiences that would detract from the teaching of the candidate or the ongoing education of Brothers within a Lodge. In addition, there were observations that many opportunities to enhance the learning of the principles of Freemasonry were missed in the way the ritual was being portrayed.

During these discussions about the practice of Speculative Masonry that occurred so freely during the meetings of the Goose and Gridiron Social Club, it became clear that many of the Brothers were interested in the way the Ritual prescribed by the Grand Lodge of Ohio could be executed in such a manner as to accentuate and highlight the learning experience.

This led to a discussion about the options available within the rules of the Grand Lodge of Ohio and its proscribed ritual and practices where meetings of "Brothers discussing Ritual" were held to explore these possibilities. As the possibilities were explored and their potential impact on candidates discussed, several things began to happen. First, members of this group would sometimes take these ideas to their current Lodges an attempt to put them into action. Unfortunately, this was generally met with great resistance and was rarely successful. As a result, the discussions began to shift toward the idea of forming a Lodge with its own charter from the Grand Lodge of Ohio to provide an opportunity to put these ideas to the test and determine their value.

This resulted in a fundamental shift in the purpose of this group from being a loosely organized social club consisting of men who enjoyed dining and stimulating Masonic discussion to a group of Brothers set on forming a Lodge in which they could implement the best practices of Speculative Masonry available to them. These were the practices that they had reviewed, discussed, and selected for what they deemed to be the best Lodge experience for them.

# Chapter 3 - Developing the Vision

The Brothers of Arts & Sciences Lodge No. 792 embarked upon a lengthy process that consumed nearly 3 months of meetings and discussions to develop and articulate a clear vision for Arts & Sciences Lodge. As with any group effort, individuals offered their talents to the benefit of the organization and, in this case, Brother Steven B. VanSlyck again stepped up to the plate with his eloquence and served as recorder and interpreter of the discussions that were held producing numerous rough drafts based upon the conversations that were held for review, refinement, and eventual adoption by the Brothers of Arts & Sciences Lodge No. 792 as their vision statement. It is reproduced here for your benefit.

## Vision Statement

> Arts & Sciences is a Lodge of Free and Accepted Masons whose members come together to bring Masonry alive in their Lodge and in their lives. We dedicate our efforts completely to the Masonic education and moral advancement of our members. In our travels, we have found that the realm of Masonic education is as boundless as human experience and that commitment to the principles of Freemasonry leads to enlightenment and personal moral advancement. Consequently, an essential requirement of membership is the cultivation of a curious and receptive mind. We care for and instruct our initiates, converse with and challenge ourselves, appreciate and respect our elders. While recognizing these distinctions, within our Lodge all but the Master are addressed as "Brother," and all stand upon the level. As a Lodge we are but one among equals. We carry the same charter, work the same ritual, practice the same principles. We strive for excellence in all we do. Our primary purpose is to create Freemasonry within the Lodge and practice it without.

You will notice that this vision statement encompasses our collective understanding about the purpose of a Lodge meeting and the expectations we have for our Lodge. By pursuing this vision, we committed ourselves to a common purpose and have rallied behind the ultimate success of this organization. One of our greatest challenges will be to bring new members into our fold and develop in them the same commitment to these ideals that we formed during our earliest days.

Brother VanSlyck has further produced a line by line explanation of the vision statement which is printed in the appendix.

# Chapter 4 - Learning the Ground Rules

Once the decision was made that we should develop a new Lodge chartered by the Grand Lodge of Ohio, a careful exploration was made regarding the procedures outlined in the Code of the Grand Lodge of Ohio. In brief, it stated that a certain number of Brothers needed to complete a specific form produced by the Grand Lodge of Ohio and affixed to it the names of the Brothers wishing to receive a dispensation to form a new Lodge and identifying its three primary officers. Appropriate fees should a company that petition for a dispensation, and a letter of support from a sufficient number of the Lodges within the Masonic District in support of the formation of this Lodge should also accompany this petition for a dispensation.

On the surface, these regulations from the Grand Lodge of Ohio seem simple and straightforward. However, in implementation, several significant challenges arose.

The Brothers wishing to form Arts & Sciences Lodge No. 792 were Master Masons in good standing from 7 different Lodges. Many of the Brothers were actively involved in their current Lodges, several of whom serving as Wardens and two of them serving as Worshipful Master of their Lodges. This gave rise to anxiety amongst the other Lodges about these Brothers withdrawing their activity from their existing Lodges to invest their energy in Arts & Sciences Lodge to the detriment of these existing Lodges. These worries were understood by the Brothers of Arts & Sciences Lodge and those of us who were charter members pledged to remain active in our current Lodges and fulfill whatever duties and obligations to which we had already agreed to avoid any damage to the existing Lodges around our district. This assurance that those who were platform officers, "line officers" or otherwise involved in their current Lodge would remain active allowed several Lodges to offer clear votes of support who might otherwise have taken steps to prevent the formation of Arts & Sciences Lodge.

Rumors and misinformation about this group of Brothers including accusations of being "elitist" began to circulate, prompting a need for a scripted presentation to be made to every Lodge in our district that would address these fears. Every Lodge was visited by someone familiar to the active members of that Lodge and the presentation offered which answered many questions that were likely to arise and provided an opportunity for those in attendance at the meetings to raise questions and have those addressed.

In addition, Brothers from various Lodges were invited to visit our informal gatherings of Brothers practicing Masonic ritual to sit and experience a "meeting" that incorporated many of the elements of the Masonic experience that we felt were important. This served to further reduce fears and anxieties about the way we would be practicing Speculative Masonry. This, too, proved to be very beneficial to our ultimate success.

Lastly, the Brother identified to be the charter Worshipful Master of Arts & Sciences Lodge No. 792 met with the District Deputy Grand Master who would be assigned to this Lodge upon receipt of a dispensation to discuss the goals, desires, and hopes of the Brothers of Arts & Sciences and to offer explanations of what we were doing and why we were doing it. When the District Deputy Grand Master would visit a Lodge in the district and would be approached with some rumor or misinformation about what was happening with Arts & Sciences Lodge, he would be well-equipped with appropriate information to dispel that rumor and correct that misinformation and assure them that all was occurring in accordance with the rules of the Grand Lodge.

We began this process in February 2009 and received all necessary approvals, documentation, and fees to submit our petition for dispensation by the end of September 2009. According to the Constitution of the Grand Lodge of Ohio, all dispensations are voided at the end of the Grand Master's term. Because the annual communication of the Grand Lodge of Ohio would occur in late October, it was decided to submit our petition for dispensation to the newly elected Grand Master once he was installed. This would allow Arts & Sciences to operate under dispensation for an entire year before submitting its request for a charter. To our delight, Most Worshipful Brother Terry W. Posey, Grand Master of Masons in Ohio 2009-2010, signed a dispensation empowering Arts & Sciences Lodge UD to operate as his first act as Grand Master on October 17, 2009. It should be noted that the directive he offered to the Worshipful Master under Dispensation was to "go forth and multiply." To some degree, it is this admonition was an inspiration for this publication.

# Chapter 5 - Implementing the Vision

Upon receipt of our dispensation, we began our regular meetings as an independent Lodge. We were now free to practice Speculative Masonry in a manner consistent with our goals while remaining in compliance with the rules of the Grand Lodge of Ohio.

We explored the rules, the opportunities available to us within the rules, as well as the various ways of presenting the ritual to maximize the learning experience for both the candidates and the Brothers in attendance. During the discussions in the formative days of the Goose and Gridiron Social Club, several key issues were brought up and thoroughly discussed in anticipation of being able to operate as a Lodge. Several of these discussions will be reviewed and summarized here to demonstrate how the concepts of the Craft Driven Lodge can be implemented.

### Size of a Lodge

Many Brothers were members of Lodges that were exceedingly large. Some had as many as 900 members in their Mother Lodge, yet rarely saw more than 25 at a stated communication. Several of these Lodges were described by their members as "degree mills" where candidates were constantly being Initiated, Passed, and Raised in a perfunctory manner with minimal education and only cursory training in the symbolism and meaning of Freemasonry. Many of these men would complete their "basic training" and never again set foot in a Lodge.

Discussions were held regarding the importance of having a personal relationship with each member of the Lodge. It was noted that if you had a personal relationship with everyone in your Lodge, then it would be easier to maintain a trusting, caring, and supportive relationship with them. To truly be available to offer aid in times of distress and to be aware of when distress was occurring and to know when aid was needed. By knowing everyone in the Lodge, anyone failing to attend the meeting would surely be missed and an inquiry made as to the reason for his absence.

The rules of the Grand Lodge of Ohio does not explicitly prohibit putting a cap on the number of members in a Lodge nor does it provide any regulations regarding this matter. Through our discussions, it was decided that we would instruct those who came after us that, when the number of members reached 50 that they were to initiate a discussion about the benefits of dividing the Lodge.

This is not meant to be a mandate to divide the Lodge. Nor does it prohibit dividing the Lodge should this seem to be a practical and beneficial choice. It was adopted as a guideline recognizing that the fundamental principle of being able to maintain a personal relationship with every member of the Lodge was an essential element of a quality Masonic experience.

Should the discussion result in a decision to divide the Lodge, then the process would begin with the mother Lodge promoting and encouraging some of its members to form a daughter Lodge. Should the discussion result in a decision to remain as a single Lodge, then the will of the Brothers at that point in time will be honored.

## Volumes of Sacred Law

Freemasonry purports itself to be nonsectarian and embracing men of any religious faith that ascribes to a firm belief in God as they understand. Throughout the experience in North America, it is rare to find any Volume of Sacred Law other than the Christian Holy Bible upon the altar. In fact, the Grand Lodge of Ohio requires that the Holy Bible be present on the altar and opened to specific places during each degree.

There are neither accommodations in the rules of the Grand Lodge of Ohio specifying the presence or absence of other Volumes of Sacred Law nor any guidelines as to how they should be handled. Consistent with the concepts of a Craft Driven Lodge, several discussions were held regarding the use of various Volumes of Sacred Law within Arts & Sciences Lodge.

The discussions noted that, in our ritual, we are told that the Volume of Sacred Law is God's gift to man to act as a spiritual or moral trestle board and that is revered place on the altar was there to provide a primary source of guidance as it functions as one of the Great Lights of Freemasonry. In addition, it is a tradition within the Lodge that no one should pass between the Worshipful Master and the altar to maintain a constant connection between the Worshipful Master and the Great Lights as a symbol of his reliance upon them for divine guidance in his governance of a Lodge.

Taking our cue from our Ritual, it was discussed about the use of Volumes of Sacred Law in several situations. Because the altar is a source of light and inspiration for all Brothers, our discussions concluded that it would be reasonable for there to be a Volume of Sacred Law on the altar reflecting the primary belief system of all the members of the Lodge. Therefore, should a member join our Lodge who practices Judaism, then the Torah would be available on the altar. Likewise, a Quran would be available on the altar should we have a member join who is a follower of Islam. This would assure that every member in the Lodge would have a Volume of Sacred Law reflecting his personal belief system on the altar maintaining equal status with the other Volumes of Sacred Law.

When new candidates would be initiated, we would ask them to provide their chosen Volume of Sacred Law and obligate them up on that text rather than asking them to be obligated on the Christian Holy Bible which is often offered as a text representing all volumes of sacred law but not specifically their own. It should also be noted that when the Holy Bible is referred to in our ritual, the wording chosen during the ritual reflects what is actually occurring in the Lodge room at that time.

Thus, through a series of discussions about the symbolic preferences and lessons attached to a Volume of Sacred Law, decisions were made to display Volumes of Sacred Law reflecting the faith of every member of Arts & Sciences Lodge.

Since the adoption of this policy, we have Initiated, Passed, and Raised Brothers of 6 different faiths and currently display upon our altar the Christian Bible, Torah, Quran, the Morals of Jesus in Nazareth, the Book of Shinto, and the Bag DaVita. Each Volume of Sacred Law has its own square and compass which is positioned in accordance with the degree in which we are opened thus completing a set of Great Lights based upon each of these volumes of sacred law.

### Progressive Line

Masonic traditions around the globe include the institution of a "progressive line" whereby a man is set on a path beginning at a particular station and progressing step by step from one position to another until he becomes Worshipful Master of that Lodge. The Brothers of Arts & Sciences engaged in a lengthy discussion about the progressive line, its benefits, and its burdens.

It should be noted that in the Constitution of the Grand Lodge of Ohio, there is no mention of a "progressive line" stating only that a man must be a member in good standing to be elected to and hold any office with the exception of Worshipful Master. To be Worshipful Master of a Lodge, he must be a member in good standing and have been elected and served as a Warden. A review of older texts regarding qualifications to be the Worshipful Master of a Lodge also provides no insight or direction regarding the existence or operation of a "progressive line."

The discussion of the progressive line, its benefits, and burdens are summarized in an essay written by Brother Daniel D. Hrinko and is presented in the appendix.

## Use of Titles

In the Entered Apprentice degree we are told that no higher honor can be conferred upon you at this or any future time. In Arts & Sciences Lodge, we interpret this to mean that the title of "Brother" is truly the highest honor available and that no title other than that is deemed necessary with the exception of the Worshipful Master who is sitting in the East presiding over the work of the Lodge.

Many of the members of Arts & Sciences Lodge have distinguished themselves within the fraternity serving as Worshipful Masters of other Lodges prior to their affiliation with Arts & Sciences, having attained honors such as the 33$^{rd}$ degree in Scottish Rite, Knight of the York Cross of Honor in York Rite, served as District Education Officers, and even having served as a District Deputy Grand Masters. Having attained such distinguished honors, they are entitled to the use of various superlatives such as Right Worshipful, Worshipful, and Illustrious.

Discussions were held on several occasions regarding the use of such titles indicating that they recognize individuals who have long labored in the quarries of Speculative Masonry and served the fraternity well. However, these titles were often used divisively to elevate one's standing among the Brothers to a position of superiority rather than accentuating the true equality that exists between all Masons who are first and foremost Brothers.

As a result, all members of Arts & Sciences Lodge have agreed to forgo any title other than that of Brother while in Arts & Sciences Lodge. This act of selflessness is an overt recognition that, regardless of your effort, service, and past accomplishments, we are all first and foremost Brothers.

This concept is further emphasized in the fact that all members wear similar dark business suits to all meetings and wear plain white aprons. The officers wear the same plain white apron as the members. Other than the position in which you are seated within the Lodge and the jewels required to be worn by the Grand Lodge of Ohio, there are no outward distinctions between Brothers.

These choices, as with all decisions in Arts & Sciences Lodge, were decided through the discussion of those members active in Lodge. It is these discussions that sets the policy, sets the direction, sets the tone, and ultimately provides direction to the Lodge administration as to what will be occurring.

# Chapter 6 – The Lodge Experience

The Brothers of Arts & Sciences recognize that a Lodge experience is more than just a meeting. A fraternal bond, like all relationships, is stronger if it is multifaceted. At one point in other Masonic degrees, it is clearly pointed out that although a single cord may be strong and a double cord stronger, a threefold cord is stronger yet. If you only see your Brothers from 2 minutes before the opening of a Lodge until 2 minutes after the closing of the Lodge, your relationship is only one dimensional and opportunities for building stronger fraternal bonds are missed.

Through the discussions that were held regarding the formation of Arts & Sciences Lodge, it was quickly recognized that multiple experiences of various types were needed to build the form of fraternal bond and contribute to the Masonic experience we all desired. As a result, we have structured our stated meetings in several parts.

## Dining

It is our understanding that dining together has been a major aspect of a quality Masonic experience since the earliest of days. The opportunity to sit, share a meal, engage in conversation, learn about each other, and to share in the happy times as well as the sad times in our lives are an essential element of the relationships we are trying to build within our fraternity. It is through these casual experiences that we are able to truly get to know our Brothers and see opportunities to develop fraternal bonds and implement those obligations of Brotherly love, relief, and truth whenever possible.

Arts & Sciences chose its current meeting location for several reasons not the least of which is the fact that a local tavern is situated 3 blocks from the Lodge building permitting us to gather for a meal before each Lodge meeting. Tables are arranged in one large banquet fashion rather than dividing into small subgroups to promote a sense of conviviality and oneness among the Brothers. The opportunity to toast successes and notable events such as the birth of a child, grandchild, and to converse about the daily activities and events of one's life is an invaluable opportunity.

These dinners also serve as an opportunity to include all the members of the Lodge regardless of the degree upon which we are working. For example, if the work of the Lodge of the evening is the passing of a Brother from Entered Apprentice to Fellowcraft, the Entered Apprentices of Arts & Sciences Lodge continue to join us for dinner anyway to enjoy a wonderful Lodge experience even though they are not yet eligible to attend the formal work of the evening. Therefore, every Brother is expected to attend every meeting regardless of their status with the Lodge.

These dinners also serve as an informal opportunity to meet men interested in Freemasonry. When a Brother learns of a person who is interested in becoming a Freemason and, upon basic investigation, learns that they may be interested in the way Arts & Sciences practices Speculative Masonry, they are invited to join us for dinner to a have an opportunity to meet many of these Brothers and to experience the Brotherly and social atmosphere we afford ourselves. While at dinner, the members of Arts & Sciences have an opportunity to question them about their motives, interests, experiences, and other essential elements as well as determining their general moral character and their desires and interests in Freemasonry. They are informed about the expectations of a member of Arts & Sciences Lodge both in terms of investment of time, finances, and the effort necessary to actively participate in the ongoing life of the Lodge should they desire to apply and be found eligible for membership. This clear expectation avoids unexpected surprises at future times or sudden changes of heart.

It is typical for someone to attend a minimum of three dinners before they are even provided with an opportunity to obtain a petition. The ongoing questions, experiences, and opportunities to discuss Freemasonry in general, Arts & Sciences in particular, and their particular goals and desires all assist us in making sure there is "a good match" between potential Brother Mason and Lodge.

Thus, our Lodge dinners not only serve as a social outlet for ourselves, but also as an opportunity for getting to know potential candidates before they even begin the formal process of petitioning.

## Social Activities

Other social activities abound. In Ohio, each Lodge is expected to complete an annual inspection which has evolved into a massive undertaking that can consume much of the energy of a Lodge for several months.

Arts & Sciences has chosen to prepare a meal for its annual inspection that involves smoking beef brisket requiring a very long day when properly done. Rather than having one Brother sit alone as the meat is prepared, Brothers who are interested are welcome to travel to the home of the Brother who is "Roasting the Beast" and enjoy various libations. The "Roasting of the Beast" has turned into a social event. The preparation of this "Beast" has created an opportunity for additional social time.

Other opportunities for social events include the Feast of St. John the Evangelist and St. John the Baptist. At the Feast of St. John the Evangelist, a dinner is held and significant others are invited at a local dining establishment. We include an educational program on some aspect of Freemasonry appropriate for mixed company. At the Feast of St. John the Baptist, a tiled Table Lodge is held at the Entered Apprentice level generally following a ceremony recommended by the Grand Lodge of Ohio or some variation thereof.

The Brothers of Arts & Sciences further explore various options through the use of alternative meetings. Twice each year, we invite nonmembers, spouses, significant others, and prospective members to participate in our discussions. A topic is chosen that is appropriate for mixed company and, following a meal together, the guests are asked to remain downstairs while the official business of the Lodge is conducted lasting no more than 15 minutes. At the close of the meeting, the guests are invited to the Lodge room to pursue the discussion topic of the evening giving each of them a sample of what Freemasonry could be about and the way Arts & Sciences practices Speculative Masonry.

# Chapter 7
# Craft Driven Decision - Making in Action

The fundamental and most essential element of the Craft Driven Lodge is the fact that every member is invited to participate in the decision-making process at all levels at all times. As a result, it is the expectation that the Worshipful Master avoids exercising his authority to make unilateral decisions unless such decisions are necessary to maintain the harmony of the Lodge or required by the Constitution, bylaws, and edicts of the Grand Lodge.

Early in the life of Arts & Sciences Lodge, we were discussing the way the Stewards moved about the Lodge room while processing with the candidate as directed by our ritual. When the Stewards reach one of the corners of the Lodge room, they must turn 90° to the right to continue their procession. Various Lodges have various traditions as to how this turn is accomplished. Some execute a wheel turn, others switch places from inside to outside, and others practice different variations to accomplish the same end. Because we had members from several different Lodges each of whom had different traditions as to how to accomplish this task, a small group of men who were discussing this issue looked at the Master and asked "Worshipful, tell us how to do this." The Master, being aware of the importance of empowering the Craft to participate in the decision-making process instructed them as follows; "Brothers, you know that our intent is to provide a meaningful experience for the candidate and the Brothers in attendance. Discuss amongst yourselves the options available, the strengths and weaknesses of those options, and choose the one you believe will be most in line with our goals as a Lodge. When you've reached a consensus, let me know."

This response is incongruent with the way Freemasonry is typically practiced. However, it illustrates the importance of empowering the Brethren to actively engage in a consideration of the options based upon the underlying principles of the Lodge. It further allows them to actively contribute to the decisions about how the Lodge should operate. Although the manner in which Stewards make a right turn at the corner of the Lodge is a trivial affair, the process illustrated in this example is critical to the long-term success of the Craft Driven Lodge. As these principles are routinely applied to the most trivial of decisions, the Brothers soon become skilled at using them resulting in their use when it comes time to make decisions regarding the most important of matters before the Lodge.

The most striking example of the Craft Driven Lodge being put in the action is at the annual meeting of Arts & Sciences Lodge. The Grand Lodge of Ohio requires that the first stated meeting in November shall be an annual meeting at which time the members will elect the officers for the upcoming year. This is a time for a

Lodge to reflect on the year that has just come to a close and to look forward to the events of the upcoming year when faced with a likely change in the administration. In many ways, it is an opportunity for a Lodge to reinvent itself and is, as a result, the ideal time for a formal process to be put into place whereby the Craft assumes their role as Board of Directors of the Lodge.

The annual meeting opens and the first order of business is the State of the Craft address delivered by the Master. This address should be a carefully considered, well written, and properly presented summary of the events that occurred over the past year in the life of the Lodge. This address should be more than a mere recitation of what happened on a factual level. It should also offer commentary on how the primary goals of Arts & Sciences Lodge, that of creating a Masonic experience that promotes education, Brotherly love, and vitality within the Craft, have been accomplished.

Specific care should be made to address those activities and events deemed to be successful and those deemed to be less than successful in accomplishing their purposes. This address should be delivered in the form of a servant to his superior on the events that occurred to provide the superior the ability to understand the performance of the servant and the impact that performance has had on the overall situation.

Following the delivery of the State of the Craft address, those who have offered their services to the Lodge in various positions are read to the membership present. Next the Election of Officers proceeds beginning with Worshipful Master.

Several of the positions within the Lodge are appointed by the Worshipful Master in compliance with the Code of the Grand Lodge of Ohio. Therefore, the Brothers of the Lodge who wish to offer their services in those appointed positions offer their names prior to the annual meeting just as those seeking elected office. At the annual meeting, a symbolic ballot is taken by the members to advise the new Worshipful Master regarding their preference as to who should fill that appointed position even though such a symbolic ballot is not binding according to the Code of the Grand Lodge of Ohio. Thus, the desires of the Craft are expressed to the Worshipful Master regarding appointments of those serving the Lodge in various positions.

The third component of the annual meeting is a discussion of the activities for the upcoming year. During this section of the meeting, an open discussion is held with all in attendance free to participate in identifying activities that they would like to see continue, discontinue, initiate, and/or modify. Brothers have an opportunity to shape the events of the upcoming year offering clear direction to the newly elected officers about what they want to see happen in their Lodge during the upcoming year. In this meeting, as the "Board of Directors" of the Lodge, the members are instructing the management team regarding the goals, responsibilities, and activities that they wish to have organized and executed during the upcoming year to have the kind of Masonic experience they desire. They are free to identify specific topics they would like to see discussed, specific speakers that could be invited to make presentations to the Lodge, or anything else consistent with the fundamentals of Freemasonry. It is through this process that the Brothers in attendance help create a Lodge that is consistent with their desires every year.

I would like to offer a personal anecdote regarding my experiences as the Worshipful Master under Dispensation for Arts & Sciences Lodge as well as being the charter Worshipful Master of Arts & Sciences Lodge No. 792.

As I would travel talking to Brothers about my experience as Worshipful Master of this Lodge during its formative years, I was often asked if I was not abdicating my responsibility as Worshipful Master because I was not setting the overall agenda, setting the tone, identifying activities, and imposing my will upon the Brothers. It was as if I was accused of failing to fulfill my duty as Worshipful Master because I was not taking total control of the Lodge during "my year" as Worshipful Master.

When confronted with such allegations, I would attempt to explain to them that my role as Worshipful Master was not to impose my will upon the Lodge, but to fulfill several important duties. The first of these duties, specified in the Grand Lodge Code, was to assure that all of the requirements and rules pertaining to the operation of a Lodge were fulfilled. This includes requirements such as meeting a certain number of times and performing each degree a certain number of times. It also requires that the Lodge comply with the rules of the Grand Lodge of Ohio regarding ballots, elections, and other matters of ritual. Lastly, it requires at the Lodge meet the expectations of the annual inspection.

I would then point out that none of these duties, outlined in the Grand Lodge Code for the Worshipful Master, had anything to do with my assuming direct control over the topics being discussed, the social activities that might be held, the fund-raising activities it might be held, or anything else of that nature. I informed them that I was a servant of the Craft one of the many, no better than anyone else, but the one chosen to organize and implement the desires of the Brethren and nothing more than that.

In some situations, this explanation would be received with curious disbelief. In other situations, I would be denigrated as failing or abdicating my duties as Worshipful Master. In a rare, few circumstances, I would receive a puzzled but positive response suggesting that this style of leadership, that of being a servant to the craft, was an idea that was unique but attractive.

# Chapter 8 – The Purpose of Lodge Meetings

A meeting is an event at which the minutes are kept and the hours are lost.
- **Anonymous**

Early in the discussions regarding the formation of Arts & Sciences Lodge, it was determined that the goal of a Lodge meeting is most clearly summed up in the Entered Apprentice lesson: we come to learn, subdue our passions, and improve ourselves in Freemasonry. This idea of Masonic Lodge meetings being a place to separate oneself from the world of the profane (those outside the Lodge) and to focus our attention and energies on "improving ourselves in Freemasonry" has been noted by various Masonic authors across time since the early days of Speculative Masonry.

The Brothers of Arts & Sciences clearly desired an educational experience and wanted to maximize this experience at every meeting. These educational experiences can take several forms. Two primary methods of education can be described as academic and collegial.

In academic instruction, a learned individual prepares a lecture, presentation, or other summary of materials to offer knowledge to those seeking knowledge in a structured format much like a modern day academic class.

In collegial education, everyone has something they can offer to those around them. Each of us, in our own way, is an expert on something and that we have the ability to share that with those around us. This system also recognizes that each of us has the ability to read, learn, and share what we have learned outside of the Lodge with those inside of the Lodge when provided with reasonable time to seek outside resources. In the collegial method, an open discussion on a predetermined topic provides an unstructured format whereby individuals can share what they know about that topic, what they may have recently learned about that topic, and ask questions of others in the room throughout the process.

To implement a collegial form of education, Arts & Sciences has embraced a model based upon the published work "Socrates Café" by Christopher Phillips. At each meeting, a discussion is held on a topic that has been previously selected and announced to the membership providing them the opportunity to explore their own base of knowledge, to consider their own opinions and questions about that topic, and to pursue other sources of information prior to attending the meeting. At the proper time, the Worshipful Master may call the Lodge from Labor to Refreshment to afford an opportunity for the discussions to be held without being burdened by traditional Masonic protocol supporting and a more relaxed, open, free flowing discussion.

The Worshipful Master or his designated representative will act as a moderator offering the question to the group regarding the identified topic as a means of starting the conversation. The moderator will also provide comments to assist the group to remain focused on the topic or question at hand rather than drifting to other topics only marginally related to the original question. Lastly, the moderator will provide a summary of many of the key ideas, opinions, and observations offered during the discussion that brings light to the topic of the evening.

On nights when degree work is exemplified, discussions usually relate to the degree or the lecture of the degree and last from 15-20 minutes. On nights when there is no degree work, discussions may last from 45-75 minutes and topics are chosen accordingly.

Every meeting has a discussion providing an opportunity for Brothers to look beyond the superficial and pursue in-depth studies every time they come to Lodge. This is a commitment made by the Brothers of Arts & Sciences to maintain its strict focus on education.

# Chapter 9 – The Agenda

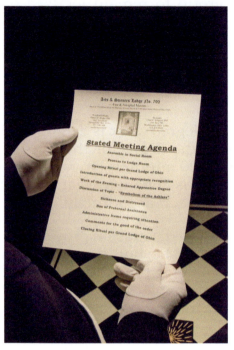

At Arts & Sciences, like every other Lodge, we recognize that no one ever joined Freemasonry for the sheer enjoyment of listening to minutes, debating committee activities, paying bills, and listening to endless correspondence. However, like all Lodges, we have certain administrative duties that must be fulfilled to support the ongoing operation of the Lodge. Minutes need to be kept, bills paid, required correspondence reviewed, committee reports to be presented, and other such actions are all necessary to the operation of any organization. As a result, we have gone to great lengths to minimize the administrative aspects of Lodge meetings whenever possible.

The Grand Lodge of Ohio maintains that certain things must be done within tiled meetings such as the reading of inspection reports, edicts from the Grand Master, and a summary of the activities of the annual Grand Lodge meeting. It also requires that minutes must be approved by the vote of the Brothers and that bills must similarly be approved by the vote of the Brothers.

In compliance with the rules of the Grand Lodge of Ohio, we have addressed several of these requirements in a way that minimizes the intrusiveness of these activities on the meeting and how are purpose.

Every year the Senior Warden, in collaboration with the Treasurer and Secretary, prepares an annual budget that is presented to the Brethren at the October stated communication. The Brothers are free to review this over the following month and can contact the authors with questions between meetings. At the Annual Meeting in November, the budget is again presented and a motion entertained requesting, *"the approval of the budget and authorizing payment of all bills contained within the budget."* Should this motion pass, it results in all bills consistent with the budget being paid without further comment, reading, or approval in a stated communication. In accordance with good accounting practices, a list of the bills paid during the previous month is included in the minutes of the meeting for review by the members. Should any member have questions about the details of the Lodge finances and expenditures, they are encouraged to contact the Secretary and/or Treasurer to discuss this matter outside of Lodge meeting time. Should an expense arise that is not contained within the budget, then it must be brought before the Lodge, discussed as necessary, and voted on separately. This has turned out to be a rare circumstance. When it does occur, a notice of the situation, the expenses involved, and the rationale for this matter is distributed to the members prior to the meeting to offer time for consideration, questions, and exploration before the meeting begins.

The Grand Lodge of Ohio requires that minutes of appropriate materials be kept and that the minutes be reviewed by the Brethren. At Arts & Sciences, we provide written copies of the minutes at dinner prior to the meeting for the review by the Brothers. Questions and comments can be made at that time and modifications made if necessary. Other options include distributing them by secure e-mail and posting them on a Lodge web site in a secure area for members to review prior to the meeting.

During the administrative portion of the meeting, the Worshipful Master states, *"Brethren, you have had an opportunity to review the minutes and a list of the bills paid during the preceding month. Are there any questions or corrections? (Pause for sufficient time for anyone to initiate any comment) Hearing none, I will ask for a motion stating that they stand approved as presented and filed for audit."*

In regards to correspondence, the Secretary makes them available before and after the meeting providing only the briefest of listing of the correspondence received and only reading those of greatest interest to the membership or as required by the Grand Lodge.

When issues arise that require planning and further investigation, such as the decision to participate in a fund-raising or social event and/or the organization of that event, a committee is quickly appointed to investigate, discuss, and make recommendations. This committee is then charged to meet outside of the Lodge time and to communicate with all the members, through the most efficient means necessary, their preliminary recommendations before the next Lodge meeting. Through this method, the ideas are formulated, discussions held, plans and recommendations made, volunteers recruited, and schedules set. These are then offered to the Lodge for a formal vote at the meeting with all discussions occurring between meetings rather than during a meeting. By implementing these procedures, it is rare that the administrative aspects of the business of Arts & Sciences Lodge take more than 10-15 minutes in its entirety.

The order of business is discretionary in that administrative business can be first, in the middle, or even at the end of the meeting. In most situations, it makes perfect sense to transition from a solemn, meaningful opening ceremony directly into the exemplification of degree work or the discussion of the topic of the evening. This is to capitalize on the focus created by the opening ceremony while our minds remain clear and focused on our primary purpose of being in Lodge, that being the practice of Speculative Masonry. In other situations, it may make sense for brief administrative duties to be conducted between sections of the degree work while the candidate is being prepared. At other times, particularly when an open discussion for nonmembers is scheduled, concluding administrative business immediately upon opening the Lodge is in the best interest of the Craft.

It is the duty of the Worshipful Master to set the agenda of the evening determining when degree work will occur, the order of business for the evening, the topic of discussion based upon the recommendations of the Craft, and the scheduling of any outside speakers or other events. In this capacity, the Worshipful Master is acting as "CEO" implementing the will of the Craft as expressed at the annual meeting during planning meetings and performing his duties being responsible for the organization and implementation of the directions of his "Board of Directors."

It is wise for the Worshipful Master to prepare this agenda well in advance of the meeting and to make it available to all the members of the Lodge through whatever means is most expedient to allow them to be prepared for the events of the evening. If the Brothers know that a particular topic is coming up that may be of interest to them, they may be encouraged to attend that particular meeting rather than to do something else. If they are aware of the fact that a particular degree is being exemplified, they may feel it is appropriate for them to volunteer to participate in a particular role within that degree.

# Chapter 10 - Ritual Work

The use of ritual is as ancient as societies. For millennia, mankind has developed ceremonial ways of celebrating important transitions in life, to honor beliefs about the ways of the world, and to create a system of structure and experiences to highlight important lessons of morality that are the underpinning of civilization.

Rituals are used to celebrate the beginnings of life as we know it, the advancement from childhood to adulthood, the transition from life as a single person to beginning of family, and the entry into various professions within the society such as that of being a warrior, Shaman, or other important trade. Rituals celebrate importance events in the life of the culture, the changes of seasons, and even the end of life as we know.

Freemasonry, like other societies, has created and adopted rituals and elevated them to a preeminent position within our society. In fact, it is the rituals that we perform and the fundamental beliefs that are communicated through our Rituals that define us as Freemasons. Although there may be variations in Ritual across cultures, countries, and across time, the fundamental beliefs and universal elements that are unique to Freemasonry pervade all forms of our ritual.

When the Brothers of Arts & Sciences began their path to forming this Lodge and defining its unique character, the ritual as defined by the Grand Lodge of Ohio played a central role in the decision making process in everything we did.

The Grand Lodge of Ohio mandates that the ritual will be performed without addition, deletion, or variation. To this requirement, the Brothers of Arts & Sciences have remained faithful. The ritual of the Grand Lodge of Ohio specifies words that must be used and, in some circumstances actions and gestures to be performed. However, in many ways, there are significant areas where individual interpretation regarding timing, pacing, and the use of illustrations can have a profound impact on the way the ritual is perceived by the candidate as well as the Brothers observing the Ritual. It is in these areas where the Brothers of Arts & Sciences have explored various versions of ritual and attempted to make use of opportunities to provide the words of the Ohio Ritual in a manner to achieve maximum educational and emotional impact on the candidate and the Brothers observing each exemplification.

The Brothers of Arts & Sciences Lodge recognize that the ritual is a profound and moving experience for the candidate and should be equally profound and moving for the Brothers in attendance. It is noted in the writings of Thomas Smith Webb that the opening ceremony should be conducted in a manner of reverence and not treated in a superficial or perfunctory manner lest the meaning be lost. At Arts & Sciences, we embrace this belief with every participant in the ritual aspiring not only to technical perfection by learning each word and delivering it as prescribed by the Ohio ritual, but developing an understanding of the meanings and moral teachings contained within those words endeavoring to deliver them in such a manner that meaning is clearly conveyed to all who hear.

As a result, great pride is taken by the members of Arts & Sciences to perform the Ritual at the highest level possible to effect a thorough communication of those moral teachings. This task, like all tasks for craftsmen who are truly masters of their trade provides an opportunity for the development of great pride and personal satisfaction at performing at the highest possible level rather than accepting adequate or even shoddy workmanship. No master of any craft should be proud of mediocre work and Speculative Masonry among all the trades, is no place for any work that is less than exemplary.

The Ohio ritual begins with a ceremony of opening a Lodge. A review of the work of earlier authors such as William Preston and Thomas Smith Webb make it clear that the opening ceremony is a ritual of transformation that allows a simple room to be transformed from an ordinary space into a sacred repose for the purpose of practicing Speculative Masonry. To this end, we approach the opening ceremonies with reverence.

The Lodge room is prepared leaving the room in total darkness with the exception of a single light illuminating the altar and Great Lights at rest. When possible, incense may be lighted to illustrate a purification of the room that will host the meeting of the Lodge and music plays softly. Music, as we are taught in the lecture of the Middle Chamber, is a way of reaching the most tender chords of the heart to enhance the emotional experiences available within the Lodge.

We begin by assembling in the anteroom outside of the Lodge room itself enjoying a time of relaxed conversation. We clothe ourselves as Masons wearing plain white aprons and donning white gloves and attend to other administrative duties such as signing the register to record those present at the evening's events.

We choose plain white aprons as a means of recognizing that all stand on the level enjoying the highest possible title of "Brother" and that other titles, although well deserved, are in no way superior to this fundamental recognition.

We choose to wear white gloves for several purposes. First, to ensure that our hands do not soil the clean white surface of our aprons allowing them to reflect the effort and lengths to which we will go to maintain our aprons in that pure and spotless manner in which we received them. A second reason for wearing white gloves is an honor to a tradition of continental Freemasonry where, by the use of gloves, the rough hands of the common laborer are masked as are the soft hands of the successful businessman or knowledgeable teacher. Thus, when exchanging grips and pleasantries, one's social station remains anonymous as we are taught that such social stations are irrelevant in determining a man's moral qualifications. A third reason alludes to the lessons of the Master Mason degree whereby we profess our innocence of wrongdoing and continue to honor our attempt to maintain such a status in our day-to-day lives.

We assemble into a procession led by the Tyler followed by the Stewards who lead to the Brethren in columns of two. Immediately behind the Stewards are the Apprentices, followed by the Fellowcraft, and they are followed by the members of the Lodge and guests. The officers then assemble beginning with the Deacons, Secretary, Treasurer, Wardens, Chaplain, and

Worshipful Master. As a procession is assembled, all become silent to reflect upon the work that is before us following the opening of the Lodge.

Several variations are available. One is to have the procession enter the Lodge by the door which is stationed in the southwest corner of the room in Ohio, and all circle the Lodge once proceeding from the door to the East by way of the North and thence from East to West by way of South and returning by way of the North following the path of the sun as it provides light to the world on its daily journey.

A second, simpler variation is to have those wishing to sit on the North to assemble in the column on the left, and those wishing to sit in the South to assemble in the column on the right. As the columns enter the room, they part West of the altar and move to the East stopping before their chosen seat and sitting when all have entered the room.

In either case, the procession allows us to move from the profane world, clothe ourselves as Masons, and enter the space where we will study and practice Speculative Masonry in an attitude of silence and reverence.

Upon arriving at the door, the Worshipful Master stops and lights a single candle waiting for all to arrive at their locations in the Lodge and take their seats.

Entered Apprentices are assigned to sit in the northeast corner of the Lodge room to maintain close contact with the rough ashlar, a symbol that represents the crude and natural state in which they have recently entered our fraternity. It also reflects their position upon their initial entry into the Lodge. They should contemplate it as a means of recalling their beginnings as a member of the profane world and the starting point of their journey through Freemasonry. Fellowcrafts are assigned to sit in the southeast corner of the Lodge near the perfect ashlar that they may remain in close contact with that symbol that represents that state of perfection for which they aspire through the appropriate use of the working tools provided them to date. Master Masons are free to sit where they choose based upon their particular preferences. Officers then retire to their assigned stations.

Upon finding their seats, all sit comfortably in silence with the illumination of the altar being the only light in the room directing our attention to the Great Lights to contemplate the purpose for us gathering. The Worshipful Master speaks the first lines of the opening ceremony and proceeds to enter the room bringing the light of the single candle into the room as it is his responsibility, as Worshipful Master, to ensure that light is added to the coming light as knowledge and Masonic education occur within the meeting of Speculative Masonry.

The Worshipful Master conveys the light to a stand in the South near the Junior Warden in whatever manner he sees fit based upon his personal form of honoring the Great Lights and the purpose of the meeting. He proceeds to his station in the East and the remainder of the opening ceremony is conducted as prescribed by the Ohio Ritual.

During the opening ceremonies, the Senior Warden is asked to satisfy himself that all present are qualified to attend the meeting about to be opened. The Ohio ritual is silent as to how this satisfaction should be met or what actions should be taken if the Senior Warden is not satisfied that all in attendance are qualified.

At Arts & Sciences Lodge, we have chosen to periodically use a procedure common in other Grand Jurisdictions to achieve satisfaction at the discretion of the Senior

Warden. This procedure, often referred to as "purging of the Lodge" and is required in some jurisdictions. However, it is not a required part of the Ritual of the Grand Lodge of Ohio. This can be done by asking the Deacons to retrieve the password and pass grip or other appropriate proof of qualification from every member in attendance and report to the Senior Warden the results of their investigation. This typically involves the Junior Deacon traveling the column on the south and the Senior Deacon traveling the column of the North going from Brother to Brother and discreetly retrieving the grip and word or sign requested by the Senior Warden.

One of our early members who assumed the position of Deacon was well respected for whispering "welcome Brother" into the ear of the Brother in attendance who had just successfully offered the appropriate grip and word. This small gesture of recognition has been identified as a warm and positive experience by many of our visitors.

After surveying both the columns of the North and the columns of the South, the Deacons report to the Senior Warden the results of their investigation and, upon being satisfied, he announces this fact and the ceremonies of the opening continue.

The lesser lights used by Arts & Sciences Lodge are wax candles that require being lit at the appropriate time prescribed in the Ritual. To accomplish this, the Senior Deacon uses an appropriate instrument to transfer the light from the single candle that was brought into the Lodge by the Worshipful Master and now resides in the South to the 3 lesser lights. The light in the South is extinguished upon successful transfer of that flame.

The Holy Bible is open to the appropriate place as required by the Ritual of the Grand Lodge of Ohio and the square and compasses are placed accordingly to the degree being opened. Each of the Volumes of Sacred Law are arranged around the altar with a square and compasses associated with each Volume of Sacred Law being placed in the appropriate position for the degree being opened.

Arts & Sciences has adopted a gesture from the practices of the Grand Lodge of Scotland by placing our right hand over our heart parallel to the floor with the thumb extending perpendicular to the floor creating a symbolic square during all times of prayer as well as the obligations of candidates. This gesture is a way of outwardly signifying that we, too, are in full agreement with the words being spoken and commit ourselves to them as genuinely and forcefully as the individual delivering the words. At the conclusion of the opening ceremonies, the Worshipful Master then proceeds to follow the agenda of the evening.

It should be noted that although the members of Arts & Sciences have voluntarily agreed to forgo any recognition of titles beyond that of Brother, all guests are afforded the appropriate recognition and honors entitled them from the jurisdiction of which they belong. Those who visit on a regular basis may choose to forgo such recognition.

Being a Lodge located in the United States of America, it is traditional that the Pledge of Allegiance be recited by all in attendance. However, in recognition that the fact that many Freemasons in attendance may not be citizens of the United States, as are several members of Arts & Sciences, we are careful to ask that the citizens of the United States join the Worshipful Master in reciting the Pledge of Allegiance rather than asking all in attendance.

If the agenda calls for the exemplification of degree work, the lighting in the room remains low and the work of the Lodge continues in subdued light. It should be noted that maintaining subdued light assures that the brightest object in the room remains the altar and the Great Lights drawing our attention to them which symbolically reinforces their central role in the practice of Speculative Masonry.

In all three degrees, when the candidate is placed at the altar, the Brothers are to form two parallel lines extending from East to West. During the obligation, the right hand is placed over the heart as described above again demonstrating that everyone in the room is again committing himself to those same obligations being taken by the candidate at that time.

At the conclusion of his obligation, the candidate is brought to light which is represented by a blindfold that is removed. The ritual of the Grand Lodge of Ohio specifies that "the lights of the room should be raised." Many Lodges interpret this as bringing all lights in the room to full brightness. From the candidate's point of view, this creates a rapid transition from total darkness, a condition he has suffered for some time, to being overwhelmed with the full illumination of the room including every nook and cranny. We recognize that such an action may not be in the best interest of the lessons being taught at the altar which is to focus our attention on the Great Lights.

We have chosen to extinguish the light over the altar at the time of the obligation leaving the room to be illuminated only by the lesser lights during the obligation. Upon bringing the candidate to light, the light above the altar is turned on thus "raising the lights in the room" in compliance with the ritual of the Grand Lodge of Ohio yet leaving the vast majority of the room in darkness. This creates an experience where the candidate, upon being brought to light is first greeted with a small pool of light that contains the altar, the Great Lights, the lesser lights, and the Worshipful Master.

As his eyes adjust, he gradually becomes aware of the two parallel lines of Brothers extending from the East to beyond the altar in the West. All other parts of the Lodge remained dark allowing the Brother to focus his attention on what is within his pool of sight that being the Great Lights, the Worshipful Master, and the Brothers of his Lodge.

This avoids introducing any other distractions that may interfere with the importance of him recognizing that these are the sources of all wisdom and goodness within Freemasonry. Through this process, we have complied with the Ritual of the Grand Lodge of Ohio while finding a way to creating more intense Masonic experience for candidate and Brother alike.

The Ritual in Ohio is broken into a ceremonial section followed by a lecture where educational information about the experiences of the ritual, the symbolisms of various actions presented during the Ritual, and a brief allusion to the meanings of the symbols is offered. The words of the lecture are a required element mandated by the Grand Lodge of Ohio and, therefore, cannot be altered, edited, or otherwise changed. However, the methods of delivery and the means of illustration are left to the discretion of the individual Lodge.

Arts & Sciences has viewed this as an opportunity to create a method of delivering lectures that is interactive with the candidate with the lecture presentation moving about the room. We make use of the objects at hand within the Lodge room to illustrate the lectures at the appropriate time. We bring in illustrations of various types be they additional objects, paintings, or tracing boards similar to those produced in the 19th century when necessary and appropriate.

Arts & Sciences Lodge makes use of lecture teams whenever possible. The Grand Lodge of Ohio does not explicitly prohibit the use of lecture teams in its ritual or code. However, caution must be taken to ensure that specific rules of your Grand Lodge or the expectations of the Grand Master and his District Deputy Grand Masters are met.

Having a group of Brothers share the responsibility of offering a lecture to the candidate has numerous advantages. First, the candidate gets to hear a several Brothers talk about a variety of things rather than listening to a single Brother speaking uninterrupted for 20-25 minutes.

Second, it affords an opportunity for more Brothers of Arts & Sciences to take an active role in the life of the Lodge by being part of a team of lecturers. It is better to have three men engaged in the delivery of a lecture with each being able to enjoy the satisfaction of actively participating in the Lodge than to have one to work very hard while two are merely spectators. This is consistent with one of the fundamental principles of a Craft Driven Lodge which is to assure that everyone has a role in the life and success of the Lodge.

A third advantage is that a Brother who wishes to take on the responsibility of learning a lecture is not expected to approach this with an "all or nothing" standard. If a Brother has learned the first three paragraphs of a particular lecture, it is perfectly appropriate for him to greet the candidate and deliver those first three paragraphs before transferring the candidate to a different Brother for the remainder of the lecture. As he learns at additional paragraphs, he can assume responsibility for greater and greater portions of the lectures. Over a period of time, it is expected that he will learn and be capable of delivering the entire lecture should occasion require. However, it is hoped that another Brother will follow behind him learning the first sections eliminating the requirement that he deliver the entire lecture in future years even though he is clearly capable.

Most Lodges throughout their jurisdictions in the United States provide a candidate with a Holy Bible or a Volume of Sacred Law of his choice to be used in the process of obligations as he progresses through the degrees of Freemasonry and to serve as a valued token and memorial of the process through which the candidate has just progressed.

At Arts & Sciences Lodge No. 792, we expect all who knock at the West gate would have a firmly developed sense of a supreme being and would already have their personal Volume of Sacred Law of which they make use at home and in their daily lives. We encourage them to bring their chosen Volume of Sacred Law to the Lodge meetings to be used at the time of their Initiating, Passing, and Raising so that this Volume of Sacred Law would serve as a reminder and symbol of their Masonic experiences as well as those other events in their life.

Instead of a new Volume of Sacred Law, Arts & Sciences presents each new Brother with a set of working tools. We found it ironic that, in the words of the ritual, working tools are presented but then physically taken from them and retained by the Lodge to be used with the next candidate. As the working tools afford the new Brother the first level of important symbols regarding the teachings of Freemasonry, it would make sense to provide the new Brother with working tools that belong to them and are theirs to take home and placed in a position of honor to serve as a daily reminder of their Masonic experiences within their home. To this end, appropriate working tools are obtained presented at each degree, and become the lifelong possessions of the Brother receiving them. This token on the part of the Lodge serves as a physical reminder to further reinforce and cement that bond between Brother and Lodge, that fraternal bond we hope to develop, nurture, and maintain throughout our lives.

## Entered Apprentice Degree

Arts & Sciences Lodge No. 792 takes pride in learning from those wise individuals that came before us as reflected in their writings. Men of great insight and talent have put pen to paper generating many documents that are invaluable in understanding Freemasonry. These documents are particularly important and useful and a Lodge such as ours which is dedicated to the education of candidates and Brothers alike.

One document of which we make use is an essay by Carl Claudy entitled "Preparation" which is given to the candidate and is to be read the day before his scheduled initiation as an Entered Apprentice. This document can be found in the appendix. In addition to reviewing this document, he is encouraged to cleanse the body as well as the spirit and to set aside time to reflect upon the journey into Freemasonry upon which he is about to embark. Through this process, worries about the day-to-day concerns, challenges at work, or other distractions can be set aside to prepare the heart and mind to be receptive to the lessons to be taught through the words and experiences yet to come.

The Entered Apprentice degree contains one particular event that is unique to it that we, as the Brothers of Arts & Sciences Lodge, have chosen to illustrate. This moment occurs when the Brother is asked for a deposit of some metallic substance. The purpose of this is to teach a lesson to encourage the Brother that he should contribute to the relief of worthy distressed Brothers when provided with an opportunity to do so if it is within his power and capabilities.

Several Masonic degrees in various bodies incorporate a similar situation in which a Brother of the Lodge either openly or surreptitiously provides resources to allow the initiate to resolve the awkward moment as part of their formal rituals. In the Entered Apprentice degree, Ohio's Ritual does not specify or explicitly prohibit such actions.

This gesture illustrates the responsibility that we are asking this Brother to adopt and clearly adds to the power of the experience and the likelihood that this lesson will be learned and retained. It also affords the candidate an opportunity to leave the Lodge room with a physical token that serves as an important reminder of this lesson which we hope he will adopt an embrace throughout his life.

## Fellowcraft Degree

The Fellowcraft degree, as proscribed by the Ohio Ritual, contains few if any unique qualities during the ceremonial section that can benefit from specialized attention to the manner of its delivery. The lecture of this second-degree as presented in the Ohio Ritual lends itself to being delivered by four Brothers. The first

Brother is free to describe the porch and pillars. The second Brother is free to describe the flight of stairs. The third Brother communicates what is necessary at the inner and outer doors, and the fourth Brother is to deliver the lecture of the Middle Chamber.

Arts & Sciences Lodge has instituted a formal, bound Roll of the Craft ledger listing all men who have joined Arts & Sciences Lodge. Keeping this Role of the Craft creates continuity with everyone who has ever joined Arts & Sciences Lodge and, if well maintained, will provide a clear sense of history among our members.

During the Middle Camber lecture, the new Fellowcraft is informed that his name will be added to the Roll of the Craft. At that point, the Ritual is paused for the Brother to enter his name in the bound book listing all who have joined Arts & Sciences Lodge No. 792.

When Brothers join by affiliation, they are required to pass a ballot by the members. After the ballot is found to be clear, the meeting progresses according to the agenda. Later in the meeting the Secretary will rise and, when recognized, inform the Worshipful Master that the Roll of the Craft is incomplete. The Brothers newly elected to be part of Arts & Sciences are then invited to report to the Secretary's desk to enter their name on the Roll of the Craft. We have allotted space for Brothers who have registered a Mark in a Chapter of Royal Arch Masons to enter their mark at this or some later time.

As with the other degrees, the ceremonial section of the Master Mason degree holds no specific or unique qualities that can benefit specialized attention in the manner of its delivery other than following the general principles of exemplary ritual work.

The lecture of the degree, as presented in the Ohio Ritual, lends itself to presentation by 2 individuals. The first section consists primarily of a retelling of the events that preceded the lecture. At Arts & Sciences, objects are left in the room and the candidate is moved about the room from place to place and from object to object as their use, purpose, and the events associated with them are reviewed. During this time, the candidate retraces his steps about the room to review and reinforce those valuable lessons presented through the experiences that had just occurred.

The other part of the lecture involves reviewing several symbols generally referred to as the "Masters Carpet" and are easily presented by a second Brother stationed at a tracing board who then provides an explanation of these symbols as well as the Masonic lessons attached to them.

In this manner, the materials presented in the lecture are done so in a manner that is engaging to the candidate and, when well presented, instructive to all in attendance.

# Chapter 11 - Candidate Education

> That which we obtain too easily, we esteem too lightly. It is dearness only which gives everything its value.
> **– Thomas Paine**

Arts & Sciences was founded with its primary goal to be the education of new and existing Masons regarding the lessons, symbolism, and implications of those lessons in their daily life. The education of candidates as men transform themselves from a member of profane society and eventually become a Master of Speculative Masonry is clearly a central part of the purpose of our Lodge. This process of education begins before any formal steps are taken toward initiating a new Brother or even petitioning our Lodge.

## Informal Visits and Dining

Upon expressing a desire or even a curiosity about Freemasonry in general to a Brother of Arts & Sciences, this man, should he appear to possess basic qualifications, is invited to attend the meals that precede our Lodge meetings. It is through these initial contacts that he is afforded an opportunity to ask questions about Freemasonry and, when appropriate, receive reasonable answers. In addition, he has a chance to experience the fraternal bonds that have been formed among the members of Arts & Sciences Lodge and see the way that guests are greeted be they Brother Mason or members of profane society. These visits also afford the Brothers of Arts & Sciences an opportunity to ask questions of the guest regarding his motives, desires, and to ascertain the level of information he may already possess about Freemasonry.

It is not unusual for men to come having already read several books about Freemasonry, its history, symbolism, and the morality that it embraces prior to making any contact with our Lodge. It is also not unusual for them to have some experience with Freemasons either through their social relationships or their family history that have left them with unanswered questions and even misconceptions. Lastly, they may have heard opinions about Freemasonry, its goals, and structure from misinformed individuals and sources causing them to have misgivings based upon erroneous information. It is during our conversations at dinner over two to four months that these issues are discussed, clarified, and opinions formed on both sides of the conversation.

If after two to four months of dinner visits and extended conversations it becomes clear to the guest that Freemasonry, as practiced by Arts & Sciences Lodge, is of interest to him and worthy of his investment of time and effort, he is free to ask for a petition. Should the members of Arts & Sciences who are familiar with the guest feel comfortable with this process proceeding further, then a petition is afforded him. It should be noted that this time of interaction is extremely informative and educational to the visitor who learns many things about Freemasonry, its purpose, symbolism, and goals through these conversations. Thus, the education of men who eventually become Brothers and Arts & Sciences Lodge begins before they even know that they are to become Brothers and Arts & Sciences Lodge.

### The Petitioning Process

The Grand Lodge of Ohio has specified a clear process for petitioning a Lodge, being investigated, and being subjected to a ballot of the membership that requires unanimity to be elected to receive the degrees of Freemasonry. Arts & Sciences Lodge fully complies with these requirements as is expected of all Lodges. Following the completion of the appropriate administrative forms, the payment of appropriate fees, the completion of the investigation process, and clearing the ballot box, a man becomes a candidate for Freemasonry and Arts & Sciences Lodge. As a candidate for Freemasonry, he is expected to participate in a school for the profane.

This process of attending the school for the profane as well as other schools at various levels is best described in the essay "From Profane to Master" by Brother Chad Simpson of Arts & Sciences Lodge which is included in the appendix.

# Chapter 12 - Developing Lodge Leadership

One lesson clearly taught through Masonic experiences is that nothing is forever and that change is a constant force at work in everything we do. Men join Lodges and involve themselves in various positions, some move into positions of leadership, and then move on to make way for those that follow behind them. This process creates an inevitable need for a continual renewal and the exploration of talents within the craft that may be used to the benefit of both the Brother and the Lodge.

To develop leadership, one must develop a thorough and in-depth understanding of Speculative Masonry as a trade. This is accomplished through ongoing education in every Lodge meeting through the exploration of symbols, meanings, the words of the ritual, related materials, the writings of those a came before us, and the implications these lessons have to us in our day-to-day lives.

A Lodge that fails to educate its members on an ongoing basis fails to create an atmosphere where leadership can be developed to the benefit of the Lodge. In essence, it results in ignorant Masons leading ignorant Masons. Such a course will surely lead to missed opportunities if not the demise of that Lodge.

This is the antithesis of all the lessons taught to us in our first three degrees. In those degrees, we are taught to learn as an Entered Apprentice, to study widely on various topics as a Fellowcraft to improve our skills, and to continually practice our trade as Masters.

Therefore, Arts & Sciences endeavors to hold discussions at every meeting and every gathering be it in a tiled Lodge room, at dinner, on social occasions, and that every other opportunity we have. These educational experiences can be formal presentations, reviews and discussions of written material, or even open-ended questions that have been plaguing us as we seek more light such as, *"what are the wages of the Master Mason that we are supposed to receive as we travel in foreign countries."*

Through this process of continually including educational experiences in everything we do, the Brothers are afforded an opportunity to continue their growth and education in Freemasonry, to expand their depth of knowledge and understanding about Freemasonry, and, therefore, are better prepared to assume the roles of leadership within the Lodge.

Leadership within the Lodge is not restricted to those formal officers that have great responsibilities in the work of the ritual. Not everyone has the talent and skill to learn and deliver ritual in a meaningful way and it should be made clear that opportunities for leadership in the Lodge should be available to those who are not so inclined. To force a man into a position for which he is unqualified will be detrimental to the man who will find the experience angering, frustrating, and possibly frightening. In addition, it will be detrimental to the Lodge who will find that the quality of his work is an embarrassment to all and detrimental to the future health and well-being of the Lodge.

Leadership can assume the form of taking numerous responsibilities within the Lodge but outside the formal roles of officers such as coaching candidates, organizing activities and events, or any other activity which contributes to the health and well-being of the Lodge. As Brothers expand their skills and talents through their study of Speculative Masonry, opportunities must be created to allow them a chance to exercise those skills. As a good Brother tells me, we should not only make but employ Masons.

## School for the Wardens

For those desiring to serve as Worshipful Master of a Lodge, it should be recognized that special responsibilities are attached to this form of leadership. To this end, the Past Masters of Arts & Sciences Lodge have established a School for the Wardens to provide an opportunity to discuss the unique responsibilities associated with serving in the East. These discussions revolve around developing a clear understanding of the role of Worshipful Master of a Lodge in general and of Arts & Sciences Lodge in particular.

These discussions involve understanding the concepts of a Craft Driven Lodge and the importance of honoring the cardinal principles of the Craft Driven Lodge that of giving everyone a voice, the ability to participate in developing the vision of the Lodge, a role in the operation of the Lodge, and the wisdom to know when to stay out of the way so that the power invested in the Worshipful Master is not used in a manner to inhibit the growth and success of the Lodge.

It is easily described in a brief review of the responsibilities of the Worshipful Master of a Lodge. His first general duty is to assure that the rules, regulations, and requirements of a Lodge as established by the Grand Lodge are followed. This task requires him to "take charge" and control the agenda as requirements and expectations are met. His second general duty is to organize the craft and the related activities such as ritual work and other events to contribute to the success of these events. This, too, requires him to "take charge" and set a calendar, delegate responsibilities, and take other actions necessary to contribute to the success of these events both qualitatively and in a timely manner.
It is important to note that the third general duty of

being Worshipful Master of a Lodge requires an entirely different set of skills that is not so obvious, difficult to develop, and often overlooked. This is the skill of knowing when to step out of the way and let the Lodge move on its own as it grows according to the desires of the craft. This involves creating an atmosphere were free communication is encouraged, attended to, and received in a respectful way. It involves knowing when to circumscribe his desires and resist the urge to "take charge" for the sake of efficiency or because "the Master knows best."

This third duty is contrary to the intoxicating nature of power and authority where we are tempted to use that power and authority in a paternalistic manner that may be judicious in the short run but lacks wisdom in the long run. To resist this urge is critical to the success and a Craft Driven Lodge and the development of this skill is the essential task of the school of the wardens.

To expand this concept further, I present the essay "On Being Master of Arts and Sciences Lodge" contained within the appendix.

# Chapter 13 - The Lodge in the Community

> Charge them to practice out of the Lodge those duties which are taught in it.
> **– Installation Ceremonies of the Worshipful Master set forth by the Grand Lodge of Ohio**

Although Freemasonry's primary and direct goal is the process of helping "good men become better," it should be recognized that this process will ultimately be reflected in the form of a positive impact in the community in which we live. It should not be Freemasonry's primary purpose to "toot its own horn" and to strive for high levels of recognition from the community for the acts that are the result of Masonic values at work within the community. Rather such positive benefits to the community are a secondary effect of these successful Lodge.

Having the Lodge actively involved in charitable works within the community also affords the Brothers of the Lodge the opportunity to see the abstract lessons taught within the Lodge come to life as they are applied in the community. Just as educational discussions that fail to connect the lessons of Freemasonry with daily life lose their value, learning moral lessons without seeing the powerful impact that can occur when they are appropriately followed within the community lessons their value and meaning. Thus, engaging in organized and charitable activities is part of the process of teaching and cementing the lessons of morality within the Brothers of the Lodge.

The process of developing, organizing, and executing a charitable event becomes a common activity that the Brothers of the Lodge can use as a means of further strengthening the fraternal ties between themselves, their Lodge, as well as each other. Working together on a committee as a team for such events will result in stronger relationships being built between the Brothers on that committee. Taking a leadership role on such a committee provides a Brother an opportunity to test and further expand his leadership skills to the benefit of himself and the Lodge.

Such activities are fully consistent with the fundamental principles of the Craft Driven Lodge. The Brothers have a voice when it comes to discussing the nature of the charitable activity to be pursued. They participate in the development of the vision about how this activity fits into the life of the Lodge. They have an opportunity to participate in a role in the Lodge contributing their talents to the overall success of the Lodge and its activities, and the leadership, by delegating these responsibilities to the committee, has supported the opportunity for the Brothers to experience their own success and the benefits of that success on a personal and Masonic level.

Arts & Sciences has decided to make Freemasonry visible within the community by taking part in several community events as Masons to increase the awareness of our existence and create opportunities for members of the profane world to ask questions about Freemasonry and its underlying principles. This can be done through open house events, fund-raising activities designed to benefit the community, or other means of exposing the community to who we are and, more importantly, what we stand for.

Arts & Sciences Lodge pursues charity both within the fraternity and within the community on a personal level. Being a young Lodge, we do not have the benefit of a large endowment or savings account allowing us to "corporatize" our giving by merely voting money from the common pool of funds belonging to the Lodge to be given for a particular purpose in done so with no particular effort on our part or any investment of our personal resources beyond those already associated with the dues of the Lodge.

The act of giving in a charitable fashion should be personal and involve direct effort and contact on our part. At each meeting, the box of fraternal assistance is passed for some identifiable charitable activity. Each Brother is free to contribute as he sees fit based upon his personal belief about that particular charitable activity. Those that share a passion for the activity can contribute as generously as their resources allow.

Arts & Sciences has established a general Community Charitable Fund which is used as needs arise within the community where our Lodge is located. To date, this fund has been used to support needs at a local elementary school, glasses for a needy family where a child was suffering in school because of an inability to see, batteries for an electric wheelchair for a Brother in distress who suffered a severe motor vehicle crash, and other similar activities. These funds are generated in various ways and all funds generated to fund-raising activities are dedicated to the charitable activities of the Lodge rather than to Lodge operations or special causes for our own benefit.

Through this process, we as individual Brothers gain the additional satisfaction of investing our effort in a cause that we find to be noble and worth our time and, subsequently, receive the rewards associated with the investment of effort. It has been said "that which is easily obtained is of little value."

# Conclusion

The concepts of the Craft Driven Lodge are as old as humanity. They are based upon those ancient qualities developed through millennia as mankind developed into a social species. Our inborn desires, needs, and the psychological forces that are part of everything we do are the power behind the success of the craft driven Lodge.

The Craft Driven Lodge provides an opportunity for each of us to explore our potentials, fulfill our desires, build relationships of value, and explore the true potential of human relationships within the structure of Speculative Masonry.

The fundamental principles recognize that we are independent individuals who, collectively, can collaborate in a trusting relationship to the benefit of all. By providing everyone a voice in the operation of the Lodge we support those principles of speculative masonry that recognize that all can contribute to the welfare of others. Through participating in a shared vision of what is to be accomplished everyone understands the opportunities that are available and how every contribution matters. By creating opportunities for everyone to contribute to success in pursuing the shared vision, personal ownership, pride, and, recognition for contributions strengthen and perpetuate the Lodge. And having Brothers assume leadership roles who encourage the principles that recognize every individual and the valuable contribution they can make, while providing structure, support, and organization sets the stage for every brother to participate in the successes of the Lodge.

These principles are, in many ways, the incarnation of the values set forth in our rituals. Those who practice Brotherly Love will allow every voice to be heard. Those who understand that leadership is a position of service will set aside personal gains and recognition for the best interest of the Lodge.

As Brothers consider these principles and explore the ways they can be applied to lodges be they old and established, young and growing, or merely in the stages of planning, is important to recognize that every lodge is a dynamic, growing, and vibrant entity with a life of its own that can grow, evolve, and adapt to continually meet the needs of its members.

Through this process, every Lodge meeting becomes a meeting where Speculative Masonry is practiced, Speculative Masonry is taught, and everyone leaves saying "this was a meeting you would not want to miss."

# Appendix 1

## The Formation of a Craft Driven Lodge; the Birth of Arts & Sciences Lodge № 792

by Daniel D Hrinko (as published in the Philalethes Journal)

Arts & Sciences Lodge No. 792 received a charter from the Grand Lodge of Ohio when it met this past October. This event was the culmination of three years of work by a dedicated group of Brothers focused on a common goal: to create a Lodge that was inspiring, enlightening, and explores Freemasonry as a philosophy.

We began as a monthly social club, informally discussing various Masonic topics. Our discussions included observations about what we felt was lacking in our Masonic experience. Comments often surfaced such as "I wish my Lodge would do more of . . ." or "Can't we spend less time reading minutes and paying bills?" or "Why do the same degree work over and over without looking deeper into what it means?"

We were all frustrated by the burdens of custom and habit within Lodge that weighed down the activities. And when asking longtime members about these "traditions," the most common answer was something along the lines of "We've always done it this way."

We were acutely aware that our time is valuable, and that spending it in dull, lifeless and uninspiring meetings is not a good use of that time. We realized that many of those seeking light through Freemasonry may be disappointed. Resolving to do something about it, we sought like-minded brethren to explore Freemasonry as a Craft, art, and philosophy through readings and discussions.

Our talks eventually included the presentation of portions of degree work, and the exploration of various ways to improve its impact on candidates. We sought to portray the ritual in a manner that would be inspiring to candidate and spectator alike. As different aspects of ritualistic work were presented and discussed, a desire to portray this work on a regular basis emerged, and the need to become a Lodge was soon evident.

We wanted to create a Lodge with meetings that we would look forward to attending, and to create a place where Masonic ritual work would be presented and discussed. A special emphasis would be placed on our efforts to understand and communicate the important lessons of the degrees. We wanted to define the term "Masonic Education" in the broadest sense, providing a forum for important topics. These discussions and experiences would support our growth as both Masons and as men. We looked forward to ultimately establishing strong social and fraternal bonds. All of this led to the adoption of our Lodge's name, reflecting the admonition of the Middle Chamber lecture to pursue the Liberal Arts & Sciences.

Essential to the construction of our Lodge was a vision, which we eventually distilled into a brief statement. We when on to adopt practices from various Lodge models so that we could implement our vision while conforming to the rules and expectations of the Grand Lodge of Ohio.

In the building of an edifice, the architect is the master who draws the plans, sets the schedule, organizes the materials and resources, and directs the work of the builders. When well executed, people marvel at the results and credit the architect with its success.

In Arts & Sciences Lodge, it is the responsibility of the Master, like the architect, to lead, direct, and organize. However, the designs he lays down must be consistent with the will of the Craft. Just as the architect must meet with the building owners to learn what is wanted, the function the building is to serve, and the qualities they find most desirable before beginning his drawings, the Master and leadership of this Lodge must meet with the owners of the Lodge, the Craft, to determine what they want this Lodge is to be. The leadership of the Lodge must identify the activities the membership desire, the qualities the Craft want the Lodge to have before any designs, including schedules, or calendar of events can be generated. After laying out the plans for the Lodge, based upon the Craft's wishes, the Master must receive the support of the brethren. They are, after all, the only resources with which the Master has to work to implement and execute the designs.

The implementation of this model requires skills on the part of the leadership to exercise prudence in their decision-making and to create opportunities for the Craft to step forward and contribute to the life of the Lodge. The process we followed involved open discussions, debates, and the developing of consensus among the members of the Lodge as to how we would go about organizing ourselves, choosing goals and directions, and implementing them. This process has been termed "a Craft Driven Lodge."

A Craft Driven Lodge is one where the ideas, goals, and will of the Craft are openly expressed to the leadership and the leadership, desiring to serve the Craft in the best way possible, takes necessary steps to bring these desires to fruition. In many ways, this way of approaching the construction and operation of the Lodge is the opposite of the model in which the Master leads and the Craft follows, and everyone in the East has "his year" and imposes "his program" on the Lodge. Such a strong tradition of leaders leading and followers following with little room for question or debate has, in our opinion, contributed to the stagnation evident in many Lodges today.

This process has been exemplified most notably in our officer selection process. Each Brother is encouraged to step forward and ask that he be trained in a particular position. A mentor is assigned; when the aspiring officer is ready, he demonstrates his proficiency in Lodge by filling that station on a pro tem. basis. At the time of elections, each Brother puts forward a list of positions in which he is proficient and willing to serve. Brothers are then free to choose who they wish to serve in the various leadership positions for the next year.

There is no expectation that a person ought to move from one position to another. The only exception to this is the election of the Junior Warden, Senior Warden and Master. The Junior Warden will be expected to move to the position of Senior Warden and, ultimately, to become the Worshipful Master serving two years in each position. This limited progressive line provides stability and predictability while the open and free nature of elections for the rest of the positions allows an opportunity for the Brothers to grow in their capabilities and serve the Lodge as their talents and resources allow.

The success of the Craft Driven Lodge depends upon the will of the Craft being expressed to the Master and officers. The Master and officers must then respond to the will of the Craft to create plans, designs and schedules. The Craft must then be willing to step forward and invest their time and effort in bringing these plans to fruition. Each year, in a sense, Arts & Sciences Lodge is reformed at its annual meeting as new ideas, directions, and expectations are set for the officers and members.

Specific activities figure prominently in our design. To build strong fraternal relationships, we gather for dinner before each meeting to enjoy socializing, introduce prospective members to our Brothers, and to welcome guests.

To make better use of our time in Lodge meetings, we reduce administration significantly. This is done by making use of committees that convene outside of the official meeting to review and gather information, and discuss items of concern to the Lodge. They then present recommendations to the Lodge as a whole in the form of written summaries and reports. All reports from committees, financial reports, and minutes from previous meetings are presented to the Craft by way of a secure section of our website, to be reviewed and evaluated prior to each meeting. Comments and questions can be addressed by e-mail and a revised copy is presented at the dinner before a meeting. Making this material available prior to the meetings eliminates the need to read the minutes in their entirety and to discuss modifications within open Lodge.

We further reduce our administration time by passing an annual budget that includes authority to pay all bills contained within the budget. Therefore, each set of minutes includes financial reports of the activities from the past month, eliminating the need for individual votes on monthly expenditures.

We set aside time for discussion in every meeting to meet our needs for personal growth and learning. Stated meetings typically involve seventy-five to ninety minutes of discussion on a topic that is selected in advance and published with the summons. This gives each Brother ample opportunity to think about, read and contemplate the topic of discussion, which enables him to arrive better prepared to actively participate in the evening's discussion.

On nights when we perform degree work, the topic of the evening always relates to the degree that was performed and twenty minutes is allowed for discussion following the presentation of the work.

All discussions are guided by the Master using the Socratic method. The Master then provides a summary of that discussion at the conclusion. Christopher Phillips' book, *Socrates Café*, is quite instructive in learning to facilitate such groups. We then published summaries of our discussions on our website, **www.as792.org**. Topics have included, *"Elements of the Entered Apprentice Charge," "The effects of Masonic Teachings and their Effects on our Roles as Fathers," "Why Was the Square Selected as a Great Light of Masonry?"* and *"How Long Is Your Cable Tow?"*

My hope in presenting this information is not to encourage all Lodges to become clones of ours. We formed Arts & Sciences Lodge No. 792 based upon our interests and needs. Our hope is to inspire others to look at the how their Lodges function, and perhaps to seek ways of supporting its evolution into a Craft Driven Lodge, where the Lodge is primarily and actively responsive to the needs and interests of its membership.

# Appendix 2

## What a Lodge Can Truly Be; The Birth of Arts & Sciences Lodge № 792, Part 2

By Steven B. VanSlyck (As published in the Journal of the Philalethes society)

Steve VanSlyck talks about the concepts underlying a Lodge where every meeting is "The meeting I wouldn't want to miss"

Part one of this article (by Daniel Hrinko printed in appendix 1) described the concept of a Craft-Driven Lodge, being one "where the ideas, goals, and will of the Craft are openly expressed and the leadership...takes steps to bring these desires to fruition." In a strict sense every Lodge is "Craft-driven," inasmuch as those who attend are satisfied, and those who are not satisfied eventually do not attend. But what the term "Craft-driven" is meant to describe is a method of self-examination and investigation, undertaken by the membership for the purpose of understanding what they want their Lodge to be. For any group to be member directed, the members must, first, see them-selves as stakeholders; second, be willing and able to take an active role in management; and third, take action.

On March 29, 2007, seven Ohio Masons broke bread in a small pub to talk things over. We had no grandiose plans. We simply wanted to share our time and talk about what we wanted from Masonry. A number of concepts and principles gelled immediately, but one overriding truth was obvious: what we wanted what we needed from Freemasonry would not be found in our grandfather's Lodge.

None of us were anything special. *"There is no doubt whatever about that,"* as Dickens would say. We were just some regular guys who happened to be Masons and who believed in the promises made to us when we became Masons.

What promises, you ask? Very simply, the promises that we would be part of something special, something fulfilling, something more – that we would be part of a search for Light, and that our brethren would accompany and guide us on that search.

Each of us have had a similar experience. We found the time spent on business, while important, hardly taxing to our intellect, and the ritual, while interesting, a Sisyphean burden we had done nothing to deserve. Shortly after becoming Masons we had all asked ourselves, what exactly had we bought into?

We discovered in that first get-together something we'd known all along: there was nothing wrong with the Fraternity. We valued the fellowship. We loved the ritual. We respected each other and the institution. We did not like the meetings.

So we continued our get-togethers as the *Goose & Gridiron Social Club*. Our motto was *"a place for like-minded Masons to gather and share good food, drink, and fellowship."* Though never expressed until much later, we knew from the outset that we wanted to be a Lodge, but that we could not adapt should not even attempt to adapt an already-existing Lodge. There was much discussion that night, but on one matter we were unanimous: we wanted to bring the after-Lodge dinner discussion into the Lodge meeting.

### A Gathering Vision

Over the course of the following two years, we took up our working tools nothing more than thoughtful discussion and an interest in learning and personal growth and considered our ideal Lodge.

We needed to define our aspirations, and acknowledged the need for a vision statement. But it had to be more than just a collection of words. It had to feel and be real. None of us were artists of the written word, but we had to identify ourselves and our goals with a statement that would truly speak to the heart of what we were attempting to do.

One of our members had seen it done before. Following that successful pattern, he suggested this beginning: "Goose & Gridiron is a group of Free and Accepted Masons who come together to bring Masonry alive in their Lodge and in their lives...." To bring Masonry alive became the goal, and the test of success or failure.

Although revised and improved continually until officially adopted by Arts & Sciences Lodge, the vision statement was read at every meeting of the social club. Because it is key to our own understanding of who we are, we read it at every significant meeting of the Lodge to this day.

But a vision statement is only a beginning. Several key concepts had presented themselves at the outset and, in time, we examined them. But we concentrated our initial efforts on the following essential points: There would be no more than three candidates per year. We would not put ourselves or our new members through the grinder. Candidates would proceed slowly and would write and present an essay before proceeding to the next degree.

We would shepherd and tend our new members, recognizing their value to the success and future of the Lodge. Candidate care and education would not be limited to the minimum requirements of our jurisdiction. A candidate would meet with three members of the Lodge and get to know them, and they him, before he would receive the first degree, and do so again with other brethren before receiving the second degree, and the third. He would be good friends with nine or more of us by the time he was raised.

Our membership would be limited to 50, and was later changed to 54. After reaching this self-imposed limit, the Lodge would sponsor and support the creation of a daughter Lodge.

Before each meeting we would break bread at a local restaurant. The stewards, serving in an office typically held by the newest Masons, would not have their enjoyment and energy siphoned away by the need to provide a meal after every meeting, and then clean up afterwards.

We wanted to adopt the English tradition of having an Immediate Past Master officer position, not to supervise the Master but to show special appreciation to an outgoing Master in a way that election as a trustee does not.

Our members would wear black suits, white gloves, and undecorated white leather aprons. Business would be handled with ruthless dispatch. Perhaps we would have a Lodge ring. There would be no special aprons or jewels for past masters. Members would address each other, including Past Masters, simply as "Brother."

And, most important of all, Lodge meetings would be dedicated to discussion. As your offer later wrote in our Statement of Principles, "the business of a Lodge is not its purpose, and it is not our purpose."

This last point, more than anything, is what could make Arts & Sciences a success, but it was not discussions meetings per se that we committed to. Our commitment was to interesting meetings, and we made that commitment and dedication to our twin principles, a covenant with ourselves and our future.

### A Vision Focused

We also studied and discussed the larger concepts on which our ideal Lodge would be based, as well as the practical issues that would arise. Each meeting saw more and more interest and focus on what a Masonic Lodge could truly be. We liked many of the new ideas circulating in Masonry. There was no rule that we had to be "this" or "that" particular kind of Lodge, so we took a little from here and a little from there, and added a little of our own.

We took our vision statement and developed its aspirations more fully, resulting in the Statement of Principles mentioned above. This document described the concepts upon which we wanted to build a new Lodge, one based on requiring a commitment from the membership of more than just time and money. The members would be expected to carry the meetings, and to make an investment of considered thought and intellectual effort in discussions to be had at every meeting. This would be essential to our success.

We worked hard to determine what "Light in Masonry" meant to us, so that we might return fair value to those who would seek it from us. We concluded that the only proper work of a Lodge is Freemasonry itself. The business of a Lodge is not its purpose. Our purpose as Masons was the search for Light, and the Lodge's purpose was to be a means to that end. To the extent permissible under Masonic law, everything else had to go.

We felt that the draw of Masonry has always been to the curious, from whom the Fraternity ideally selects those who are sincere in their desire to learn. Men who experience our degrees but do not return have found more compelling interests. First and foremost, we decided, Lodge meetings must be made interesting. To attain this goal, we did nothing more than focus on our twin principles of Masonic education and moral advancement.

These two principles are the pillars of the Royal Art, and an essential part of the initiate's search for Light. As we understood it, the fundamental goals of Masonry were to build a foundation for personal growth (Strength), to educate and enlighten one's mind (Beauty), and to seek moral advancement (Wisdom).

Our plan was to explore these principles through discussion. From the day the Grand Master signed and sealed our dispensation until now, there has not been a single meeting of the Lodge in which some topic focused on Masonic education or moral advancement was not presented and discussed, including our annual meeting and every degree presentation or conferral.

We believe that those who knock on our door are desirous of being brought to Light. Indeed, the very word "petitioner" reminds us that candidates come to us seeking something and rightly or wrongly, they do so with expectations. None of these expectations could be more reasonable than that of receiving what Masonry has promised a path to Light. To us, the search for Light offered, nay required, much more than typical Masonic education programs had on offer. Such a search required a conscious decision to explore morality. That we might be serious about moral advancement, we decided our meetings should naturally include the study of ideas and aspects of life which make us uncomfortable, and these studies should naturally cause us to examine and reexamine our opinions and judgments. No topic would be deemed inappropriate provided it could be offered and approached with due regard for Masonic harmony.

The exploration of morality would be company by general Masonic education as well. We concluded, however, that the Arts & Sciences which ultimately include nearly every subject provide an inexhaustible fund of knowledge ready and waiting for the curious and receptive mind. Some may find this "all learning is Masonic learning" idea uncomfortable, but we do not. As renowned Masonic scholar Trevor Stewart documented in his 2004 Prestonian Lecture, such an approach is entirely consistent with the practices of classical Freemasonry, for it was once common for Masonic Lodges to host lectures on a wide variety of subjects. After all, as William Preston himself wrote in 1788, "Masonry comprehends within its circle every branch of useful knowledge and learning." Accordingly, the universe of Masonic topics is no more limited than the collective knowledge of mankind.

## A Vision Realized

When our club began walking more surely down the path of obtaining a charter, we took care to keep the Grand Lodge informed of our activities, even to the point of requesting permission to rehearse the ritual in a proper setting outside of a tyled Lodge. In February of 2009, after two years of meeting as the Goose & Gridiron Social Club and with a Past Grand Master in the chair, the club members selected a Lodge name and voted to seek a dispensation. It was granted at Grand Lodge the following October.

In part one of this article, our Master described many of the procedural matters we settled on during our year under dispensation. Some of the suggestions may seem familiar, such as having a budget, letting interested brethren serve in officer positions pro tempore, and so on. We make no special claim to originality in any of this. We only claim a love of the Craft and a willingness to give the ideas discussed above a serious and real chance to work. The result is a Lodge whose meetings none of us wish to miss.

The lion's share of meeting time in Arts & Sciences Lodge is devoted to discussion, facilitated by the Master. This is one of his most important duties. Part one mentioned the Socratic method, but we do not engage in challenge questioning. A meeting may be a series of comments, or in the nature of a conversation, or carry whatever aspect of discourse works best at the time - but we always "meet upon the level and part upon the square."

However the discussion progresses, the Master's responsibility is to encourage reasoned argument and vigorous participation so as to fully develop the topic and any significant tangents. If we as a Lodge both require and allow him to do so, we will meet our stated goals and no member will go home without having learned something new about his universe, or without having viewed someone or something in a new light.

Arts & Sciences Lodge is an experiment, not an experiment with Masonry, for we do not believe that experimenting with Masonry is particularly useful. Rather, we are an experiment with an idea: that the individual member can leverage the power of his Lodge to make Masonry a constructive and useful force in his own life. It is to that end that we have been called to labor.

# Appendix 3

## Statement of Principles of Arts & Sciences Lodge

by Steven B. VanSlyck

### Introduction

Arts & Sciences Lodge is an experiment. Not an experiment with Masonry, for we do not believe that experimenting with Masonry is either appropriate or useful. Rather we are an experiment with an idea: that the individual member can leverage the power of his Lodge to make Masonry a constructive and useful force in his own life.

We believe that those who knock on our door are desirous of being brought to Light. Indeed, the very word petitioner reminds us that candidates come to us seeking something—and rightly or wrongly, they do so with expectations. None of these expectations could be more reasonable than the expectation of receiving what Masonry has promised—a path to Light. We have, therefore, worked to determine what Light in Masonry means to us, so that we might return fair value to those who seek it from us. In doing so we have concluded that the only proper work of Masonry is Masonry, and that the Lodge is an obvious venue for teaching that work. Our thoughts about how to do this are summarized in the Vision Statement presented above and explained in the pages that follow.

If our experiment of a limited membership, slow growth Lodge whose meetings focus on discussion rather than administration results in Lodge meetings which draw the members, then we can ask no more. It will be for others to judge our success.

"Arts & Sciences is a Lodge of Free and Accepted Masons..."

We are a Masonic Lodge, erected to God and dedicated to the Holy Saints John. As a Masonic Lodge, we work under the auspices and guidance of our Grand Lodge, make Masons, follow the landmarks and tenets of Freemasonry, and try to pass on what we learn to those who will follow. As a Lodge of the Holy Saints John, we seek to both gain knowledge and attain wisdom, and we focus our efforts in those endeavors.

> "...whose members come together to bring Masonry alive in their Lodge and in their lives."

Bringing Masonry alive requires, first, a shared vision of what Masonry is; second, a set of defined goals against which to measure progress; and third, a plan for attaining those goals. The purpose of this booklet is to outline these concepts and provide proper instruction on how we might go about this work.

In terms of what Freemasonry is, there may be no better answer than the sort given to a potential member: Freemasonry is a fraternity of honest and respectable men who believe in God and desire to associate with each other for the purpose of personal improvement and moral advancement.

Believing that no man is perfect and, therefore, that personal improvement and moral advancement are attainable only to the extent by which we continue to strive for them, we submit that our fundamental duties as Masons are:

- To build a foundation for personal growth (Strength),
- To educate and enlighten our minds (Beauty), and
- To seek wisdom and moral advancement (Wisdom).

These are our goals.

In the several Masonic degrees we learn about the twin pillars at the entrance to the porch of King Solomon's Temple. A Mason entering our ideal temple passes through a porch framed by what we might call the twin principles of Masonic education and moral advancement. In our view these twin principles both establish the foundation upon which our Lodge might best be built, and provide the framework for a strong and virtuous temple to be erected thereon.

> "We dedicate our efforts completely to the Masonic education and moral advancement of our members."

Masons form Lodges for many reasons. The members of our Lodge have an ideal—or idea—of Masonry based on the twin principles described above, just as we imagine that Masonic Lodges of 200 years ago may have been. Whether this belief is factually accurate or not, for our purposes anything which does not directly contribute to the education or personal moral growth of our members is seen as a distraction and therefore secondary.

> "In our travels, we have found that the realm of Masonic education is as boundless as human experience…"

The draw of Masonry has always been to the curious, from whom the Fraternity ideally selects those who are sincere in their desire to learn. Those who are initiated, passed, and raised but do not return have found interests elsewhere. So a Lodge meeting must first and foremost be interesting. This need not be a difficult goal to attain. We need do nothing more than focus on our twin principles—both of which are informed by learning, whether the present object be intellectual improvement or moral advancement. These are the essence of the Royal Art, which is, at bottom, a search for Light.

The search for Light is, in fact, the very reason we sought to become Masons. Obviously, therefore, Masonic education should be a priority in our Lodge. It should take center stage, and a broad stage it should be. Moreover, an education program is not Masonic simply by being topical of Masons, Masonry, or Masonic symbolism, and is not educational if the mind is not engaged.

Members of our Lodge should expect a genuine educational experience, lively discussion of any area of knowledge under the sun, a whetting and satisfaction of their appetite for more light. It is our obligation to provide it. This is not in derogation of any Masonic education program. Indeed, it could not be, for education, however styled, draws on unlimited resources and has been a central purpose of Freemasonry, and the primary object of her Lodges, for centuries. To our minds, therefore, Freemasonry and learning should be synonymous terms. Masonry is education.

When our educational programs are not ceremonial, they should, with due regard for Masonic harmony, be unlimited in scope. The objective of education is, after all, no more limited than the collective knowledge of mankind. Public servants; military officers; master tradesmen; scientists; doctors of divinity, medicine, law, and philosophy—all of these should be regular and customary speakers and discussion leaders in our meetings. The Arts & Sciences provide an inexhaustible fund of knowledge ready and waiting for the curious and receptive mind. No member should go home without having learned something new about his universe.

> "...and that commitment to the principles of Freemasonry leads to enlightenment and personal moral advancement."

Personal moral growth is the most challenging of human endeavors. Rationalized on the one hand by *"I don't need it"* and on the other by *"I don't want it,"* every objection to doing the work required for moral advancement boils down to fear. But fear's only child is closed-mindedness, and a closed mind is anathema to learning. William Paley wrote about closed-mindedness in his 1794 work, *"A View of the Evidences of Christianity."* In 1879 some unknown writer condensed Paley's words to a single sentence, which, slightly modified, was later attributed to the great philosopher Herbert Spencer as follows:

"There is a principle which is a bar against all information, which is proof against all arguments and which cannot fail to keep a man in everlasting ignorance—that principle is contempt prior to investigation."

If we are serious about moral advancement, it follows that our meetings should naturally include the study of ideas and aspects of life which make us uncomfortable, and that these studies should naturally cause us to examine and reexamine our opinions and judgments. Moral advancement is the proper and primary work of a Mason, whether experienced by participation in the rites of Masonry or by discussion in Lodge about the nature of right and wrong, good and evil. And as any man who has found a path to moral advancement will testify, the humility gained by the effort alone becomes its own reward as it slowly opens the heart to the whispered good counsel of that "still, small voice within." No member should go home without having viewed someone or something in a new light.

> "Consequently, an essential requirement of membership is the cultivation of a curious and receptive mind."

We recognize that some will find our customs appealing and that others will not. Freemasonry offers many paths for those who seek more light. The path we offer—which focuses in part on education, discussion, and even debate - will draw the interest of those who enjoy such pursuits. Prospective members who find value in these principles, and who enjoy the give and take of thoughtful conversation on topics which might be brought before the Lodge, will find our meetings pleasurable and, we trust, even exciting. But a desire to learn, to consider all sides of an argument, will be indispensable.

But what applies to prospects applies to members even more. A "curious and receptive mind" is an open mind, one well suited to learning. Not for nothing does the Fellow Craft Degree center on the liberal arts, "that valuable branch of education which tends so effectually to polish and adorn the mind," for only by continually improving the mind may we more fully discern and thereby appreciate the works and intentions of the Divine Artist. Accordingly, each member's desire to learn, if given free rein, will enhance the Masonic experience for all.

> "We care for and instruct our initiates,…"

*Care for,* as in shepherd. The failure of a candidate to advance in the understanding of Masonry is our failure, not his, and each member of our Lodge must take it as a personal point of pride to aid and welcome our new Masons and assist in their advancement. This may require practice using the telephone, or the steering wheel, or otherwise require us to go out of our way for the new member.

The new member is the most important person in the room, and should find himself attended by interested and friendly brethren at all times. This must be clearly understood—and practiced—by every Master Mason. The prospective member, candidate, Entered Apprentice, Fellow Craft, and even visitor have a right to be shy. The rest of us do not.

*Instruct,* as in train up the mind. Building on the foundation of the Grand Lodge's candidate instruction program, we must also understand and fulfill our greater duty to the initiate: to inspire curiosity and wonder, to nurture those traits along, and to see them bloom. And while we expect more from our initiates than simply learning the basics, we encourage them by being sounding boards and providing guidance, not by being walls to new ideas, providing pat answers, or parroting concepts into which we have not ourselves invested due mental effort.

> "...converse with and challenge ourselves,..."

The only real contention among Masons should be "that more noble contention, or rather emulation, of who best can work and best agree." A structure is said to agree when it is plumb, square, and level and its several parts fit each other as originally conceived and properly designed.

But a spiritual temple no more builds itself than any other structure does. And we must be assured that the tools with which we build our spiritual temple are kept in proper order. The discussion in our meetings may seem at times to be overly enthusiastic or even undisciplined, but we struggle as Brothers in a war against mental laziness and moral self-satisfaction. We may probe, and question, and disagree, and otherwise test ourselves, but when we keep our Brother foremost in our mind, we will meet our goal of providing a Masonic experience valued by our members, and the Lodge will never close in disharmony.

In challenging each other we never object for the sake of proving our Brother wrong, nor to prove ourselves right. We challenge our own and our Brothers' understanding of facts, processes of thought, and conclusions reached not only to sharpen and improve ourselves but to raise up our Brother likewise, that his own thoughts, his own moral stature, his own temple, will be of the highest possible quality.

> "...appreciate and respect our elders."

From mistakes comes experience; from experience comes wisdom. Whether by circumstance, age, or providence, our elders have faced challenges, solved problems, and gained hard-won insight from experiences youth has yet even to imagine. Wisdom cannot be taught, but with an attentive ear it can perhaps be learned. Willingness to receive instruction, and due effort at understanding the lessons offered, is key. Paraphrasing the greatest ritual writer in modern American Freemasonry, *"We have reached the age when we may be prone to forget the sacrifices made by those who have preceded us. But no virtue so becomes a man who, gratefully remembering the debt he can never repay, strives to pay it nevertheless."*

If it were not for those who preceded us, there would be no such thing as Freemasonry. We must keep this simple fact in the forefront of our minds, for it is our responsibility to pass the light of Masonry to those who follow.

We will therefore extend a curious and receptive mind to our elders just as we would to any other. More than this, we will aspire to selflessness with our time. The world has no wealth at all but what is found in the human heart, and the coin of that wealth is the time we give in service to others. Let us give of our time - to our elders and to all - *"without let or hindrance."*

> "While recognizing these distinctions, within our Lodge all but the Master are addressed as "Brother," and all stand upon the level."

Men who work for their achievements in life are justly entitled to the fruits of those labors. The same applies in Masonry. Among ourselves, however, we have made a personal decision to recognize no special distinctions apart from that given to the Master, who, though "temporarily chief among his brethren, has only emerged for a brief time from the ranks, and to the ranks will soon return." This is not to suggest or justify discourtesy, but to better encourage conviviality and personal friendships among our members, and to recognize that in this life we are but Fellow Crafts engaged in the work of building our individual spiritual temples, Masonry being one place where we learn how to execute good work, true work, square work.

Courtesy is no sin, and hospitality is a duty enjoined by God. Both are indispensable to the work of Masonry. As we do with our initiates, we welcome visitors warmly, keep them company, and endeavor to make them feel at home. If they have labored in a Right Worshipful Lodge and been inducted into the Oriental Chair, they are entitled to be addressed as "Worshipful," and we recognize them as such. We do not impose our internal customs and traditions on our guests unless they have elected to embrace our ways and subscribed to these principles.

It should be remembered, further, that neither the Grand Master nor any other Grand Lodge officer, including a Lodge's supervising deputy, ever visits a Lodge other than in an official capacity. These brethren shall be addressed in the forms to which they are entitled and received with full honors on every occasion. We will not embarrass either the Lodge or a visiting dignitary by asking if he wishes to be introduced or how to do so.

> "As a Lodge we are but one among equals."

Every regular Mason does, by right, claim membership in what has for centuries been an elite assemblage. But although there are three degrees, there is no preference among Masons. Just as we should treat each other with humility within the Lodge, so should we act with humility as a Lodge. We are not *"first among equals."* That is the prerogative of the Grand Lodge and the Grand Master. We are not *"better than"* any other Lodge. We do not *"know more"* than any other Lodge. We do not do things *"the right way"* compared to other Lodges. We have no pedestal upon which to stand. We do, however, have goals we have set for ourselves and responsibilities both to ourselves and to others. Directing our efforts to those ends will be to the benefit of all.

Peculiar requirements of our Lodge, such as our regular festive board, standard apron, dress code, wearing of white gloves, membership limits, and similar policies, have been put in place to remind us that success requires personal commitment—that Masonry is a privilege, and that her real benefits are bestowed only upon those whose working tools are employed in the proper work of the Craft. We therefore view Masonic membership as carrying obligations, not rights. On no occasion shall we ever require or pretend to special treatment, special circumstances, or special privileges.

There is one claim we should wish to make, if it can be made honestly: *the claim to interesting meetings.*

Our members come seeking Light. It appears obvious, therefore, that when we are not executing or perfecting the Work, our meetings should consist of education in art, science, and philosophy. Ideally, the role of the Master will, at these times, evolve to include being a discussion leader, moderator, or perhaps even referee as the members themselves take the argument - in the classic sense - wherever it may go. However it may be done, an effective Master will create an environment which encourages and even demands participation and discussion.

Our meetings are to serve our members. Nothing should be done in Lodge that is not required by Masonic law to be done in Lodge unless it directly advances our goals of Masonic education and moral advancement. All business of the Lodge which can lawfully and properly be deferred to committees shall be so deferred. Committees shall meet as often as necessary to do their work, and those who are interested in the "business" of the Lodge are invited and encouraged to participate in and attend their meetings. But the business of a Lodge is not its purpose, and it is not our purpose.

The majority of every meeting shall be devoted to Masonic education. When this education does not consist of a degree practice or conferral, it will, with due regard for the demands of harmony, be without limitation as to topic and conducted in such a way as to encourage reasoned argument and vigorous participation.

> "We carry the same charter, work the same ritual, practice the same principles. We strive for excellence in all we do."

We are a chartered symbolic Lodge working under the authority of the Grand Lodge of Free and Accepted Masons of Ohio. Within the strictures of the Old Charges and the Code for the Government of Lodges we have a great deal of freedom, and we will exercise it responsibly. As a Lodge we shall endeavor at all times to be a role model. As individual members we will keep in mind that our Lodge will be judged by our personal behavior, and we will act accordingly.

Finally, and as we all know, anything worth doing is worth doing well. While no one is perfect and perfection is, by definition, an impossible standard to meet, continued study and improvement can be and often is a reward in itself. Our intentions here are no different from anyone else's. Only our methods may differ, to a greater or lesser degree.

Aspiring to a high standard, our credibility is always on trial, and continued study is the best assurance of credibility. We will strive, so far as we can, to speak credibly or not at all, laboring all the more strongly in this as we advance in rank, station, or years.

In matters of ritual and Masonic law, our books will be well used, their pages turned and turned again. We will take especial care to avoid "knowing the answer" to any question of Masonic law or ritual unless we have our homework in hand. Nor shall we suggest to our superiors that they do our work for us. A request to a superior for guidance should always be accompanied at the least by some reference to the applicable instruction or rule.

Only by listening to our fellows regardless of their station, by reading the instructions others have so laboriously penned for our use, and by having due regard for those with special expertise will we be assured not only of competence but of real quality and even excellence in our own work.

> "Our primary purpose is to create Freemasonry within the Lodge and practice it without."

This is the purpose of every Masonic Lodge, the purpose of the principles described above, and "a consummation devoutly to be wish'd." Our simple desire is that we might "practice without the walls of this, our invisible college, that which we have learned within."

# Appendix 4
## Preparation

by Carl Claudy
Printed in 1925 by the Committee on Masonic Education and Service for the Grand Lodge, A.F. & A.M. of Texas, and mentioned in the May 1926 Short Talk Bulletin, "truly prepared."

You are preparing to become a Freemason. How are you preparing? You have the ambition to put on your breast a tiny pin representing the square and compasses; and ambition to be known as a master Mason; and ambition to join the great fraternity of which perhaps your father was a member; and ambition to be one of the large Brotherhood of which you may have heard so much and of which you know so little.

So you asked a friend, whom you knew to be a Freemason, how to proceed. He gave you a petition to fill out and sign. You were asked to declare your belief in God, and probably your friend explained to you that *"God"* here means the supreme architect of the universe, call him walk by name you will. He may be to you God or Jehovah or Adonai, or Allah.... It makes no difference to Freemasons by what name you call him, so long as there is within you the humble acknowledgment that you are creature of his, and that he reigns over the heavens and the earth.

It is all very simple; the other questions are of a practical and mundane character, and give you no hint of what a degree may be, and what sort of the ceremony of initiation you will participate, what kind of a fraternity Freemasonry is.

And so there was no hint given you in the paper you signed as to what sort of preparation you should make to become a Freemason. Freemasonry jealously guards her reputation, which is of humility and self - a face meant as well as of secrecy and good works.

Freemasonry does not advertise herself. Her contacts with the world are numerous and commonplace, she works so silently, so quietly, that the world knows little of her labors. You seldom hear Freemasonry discussed in public, and references to Freemasonry in the literature of all countries are so cunningly concealed, that you, and all others not members of the craft, have almost nothing to guide you as to what you should do to and for yourself before you take your entered apprentice degree.

But if you seek, you shall find, in Freemasonry as well as elsewhere. If the friend to whom you went for your petition is a well-informed Freemason-and not all good Freemasons are as well informed, or as articulate about what they know, as you might like-he will tell you certain things. In case he cannot or will not speak, some of those things are set down here.

You asked a friend to take your petition into his Lodge. His Lodge is his Masonic home. Around the cluster all those happy memories, all those beautiful thoughts, all those heart-searching experiences, which go with the word "home." You asked him, therefore, to pay you the complement of taking you into one of the sacred places of his life; in the hope that it will be, and the implied promise that if admitted it shall be, to you one of the sacred places of your life.

You asked not a stranger, but a friend for this. In his first reply was to direct you to express yourself as to your belief in God.

It does not take a very clever man to see that with such a beginning-the call of friendship, the sacredness of home, and the belief in God-Freemasonry is not a joke, not a foolish fun organization, not a club of "good fellows"; and not an organization to join as one would a board of trade, for business purposes. It is obvious to anyone who thinks, that Freemasonry must be dignified, beautiful, impressive, that it must have a real meaning, a real part to play in a man's life.

Therefore, Brother to be, make your preparations to become a Freemason as you would prepare for any other great and enobling experience of life.

When your petition was signed and delivered, the matter was out of your hands. The Lodge assigned a committee to ascertain if you are worthy, from their standpoint, to be of the Lodge. Your name was voted on, in due time. You were elected. Now you are notified to present yourself at the West gate for initiation.

When you go, go clean in mind, in body, and in heart.

Take from your mind and cast away forever all thought that there is a *"Lodge goat"* awaiting you, or that your friends are going to "have fun with you." There are fun-loving organizations which cast aside solemnity and spend most of their evenings and laughter and play. But in a master Masons Lodge, never! There is not a word spoken, and action performed, which can hurt your dignity or your feelings; there is no torture, physical or mental, to degrade you or Freemasonry. There is no *"horseplay"* or other unhappiness awaiting you.

What is done with you has a meaning; the part you play is symbolic, and intended to make a *"deep and lasting impression on your mind"* of truths, the full understanding of which make you a better man. Put all fear from your mind; remember that it is among friends you go, and that the first question they asked you was of your belief in a common father; men do not start those who begin to play a joke.

Go clean in body, as you would go clean to a christening or a baptism. Nor present this instruction here; there is intended no insinuation you are not always clean. But go made clean expressly for this ceremony; though you have but just come from the bath for the evening, go once more and bathe with the thought that you are preparing now for a great step, that the water which leaves your body is also, symbolically, cleansing your mind in your heart. Put on your freshest linen, and let its thoughtlessness be symbolic of that spotless this your thoughts should have. For if you neglect these things you will be sorry, afterwards; what Freemasonry does to you is done to you, not your Brother and that will be, and Freemasonry will mean more to you as you approach her altar humbly and purified.

Finally, Brother to be, go with a humble and contrite heart. If it is in your power to do so, put from your heart all evil. If you have an enemy, make an effort to forgive him before you enter the portals of the temple. If you have done a sin, do your best to honestly regret it before you pass to the West gate. If you have wronged anyone, make up your mind to right the wrong; you will be the happier man who later in the evening if you do. And just before you leave your home, go alone in a quiet room, and, all unashamed, get up on your knees before that God in which you believe, and ask his blessing upon that which you are about to do. Pray humbly for the width to understand what you are about to hear. Ask that it may be given to you to be a good Freemason, to be a Brother to others who will be Brothers to you, a real workman in the quarry, erecting to him a temple not made with hands.

So shall you become an entered apprentice with the greatest benefit to your Brother, and real joy to yourself.

# Appendix 5

## The Progressive Line in Freemasonry: Its Benefits and its Burdens

Daniel D. Hrinko, W.M.
Arts & Sciences Lodge № 792
Grand Lodge of Ohio

One of the founding principles of Arts & Sciences Lodge was that all of the many aspects of Freemasonry should be investigated and discussed as a means of gaining further light about their importance and the lessons they contain. This should be done in a thoughtful and conscientious manner just as every topic deserves.

Through our experiences in other Lodges, our members have had extensive experience in the officer progression process typical in our Lodges, a model generally referred to as the "progressive line." We felt that discussing the benefits and burdens of this model was an important step in our development as a Lodge.

What follows is a summary of the salient points which our discussion revealed and is, accordingly, the product of many brilliant minds; not of any single one. Your writer's role was merely to compile this summary.

Our discussions revealed that a benefit of the progressive line model was to provide a system for training men to become proficient at the tasks associated with various positions within the Lodge. It can assist them in learning the ritual, familiarize them with their administrative and leadership duties, and prepare them to undertake their responsibilities in a manner in which they can take pride.

Specifically, the progressive line model and set a path or standard of expectations which encourages the member to invest the time needed to learn what is required to be successful in the tasks he is expected to fulfill. It provides a sense of continuity in that one knows what is expected of him, now and in the future.

It provides a means of avoiding stagnation whereby certain positions may be filled by the same person for years on end, to the detriment of the Lodge. It creates a structured opportunity for new members to assume responsibilities. Lastly, it sets the stage for nine or ten members to be active in nearly every meeting.

However, our discussions soon identified several problems, or at least perceived problems, associated with this model. The progressive line forces qualified Brethren to move out of a position and, eventually, out of the officer line, denying the Lodge the direct benefit of their expertise and talent. It creates a rigid system whereby people are prevented from moving into or out of officer positions. It sets the expectation that once you enter "the line," you are expected to fulfill all duties of all offices for the next several years whether you are willing or not. Each officer is expected to move up and out, and in lockstep.

It also creates the expectation that a Brother must be an officer to be involved in the Lodge's activities, and if not an officer, then he is to be merely an observer on the sideline. Just as it establishes the assurance that nine or ten members will be active in nearly every meeting, it likewise creates the limitation that only nine or ten members will be active in any particular meeting.

There are times when this model breaks down, such as when a Brother is forced, by job or other commitments, to drop out, creating a hole in which either a past master or an unprepared Brother must then be placed. It sets the stage for viewing one who is forced to leave as letting the Lodge down at best, or at worst as being disloyal. Finally, it creates a situation where one who lacks a commitment to excellence will do only the minimum necessary to progress, and everyone around him must then compensate for his shortcomings.

In our discussions of the options available to us, we began with the rules of the Grand Lodge of Ohio applicable to officer qualifications. They were straightforward and clear. The Code for the Government of Lodges states that to be installed as Master of a Lodge, a Brother must have first served as a Warden, and received the Degree of Past Master either in a Convocation of Past Masters or a Chapter of Royal Arch Masons. In the ancient charges, as published in the Constitution and Bylaws of the Grand Lodge of Ohio, we learn that "the most expert of the Fellowcraft shall be chosen or appointed the Master or overseer of the Lord's work; who is to be called Master by those that work under him." Beyond the progression from Warden to Master, the concept of a progressive line is nowhere to be found.

Since there is no requirement of a progressive line, we then discussed alternative concepts, methods or ways of preparing and selecting officers. Having "a free for all" election for every position would make it difficult if not impossible for the Lodge to have stability, predictability, or address the need for preparation. We noted that truly open elections create opportunities for qualified brethren to take on responsibilities as their interests and talents allow rather than being forced into a set system. Those who have the talent and ability to move into positions of authority quickly while serving with a high degree of proficiency can do so. Those who possess other talents or have no interest in the senior level of leadership are free to apply their energies in ways useful to the Lodge but more fulfilling to them.

Clearly it is important to the welfare of any Lodge that all our brethren have opportunities to learn, master, and demonstrate their proficiency at whatever position may interest them. By providing such open opportunities through open elections, we set the stage for growth within our Lodge. But each opportunity we create brings on a new challenge: How do we identify those willing and competent to serve in office?

Our discussions lead Arts & Sciences Lodge deciding to pursue a blended system. We concluded that the Junior Warden, Senior Warden, and Master would be considered the "progressive line." This would bring the benefits of continuity and stability to the Lodge's senior leadership. We created a mentorship system to provide training opportunities for interested members to serve the Lodge as officers, and as a means for demonstrating proficiency. To further improve stability, a consensus of our members favored having the Master and Wardens in their stations for two years.

This mentorship system expects a Brother interested in a position to show initiative by approaching the mason serving in a particular office and, expressing a desire to learn that particular position, spend time with that officer learning the ritual and the responsibilities of the office. When he is ready, he will volunteer to pro tem that position over the course of several meetings to demonstrate his proficiency. Should he be interested, motivated, and talented, any Brother may have the opportunity to learn and demonstrate his proficiency at several positions during a particular year.

This mentorship model allows as many as are interested to be actively involved in nearly every position in the Lodge without formally accepting the responsibilities of being an officer. The model allows the brethren to be involved and contribute to the life of the Lodge in a way which allows flexibility and is limited only by their individual motivation and talents.

The mentorship model also expects the officers to encourage members to study with them and become proficient at those positions, eventually stepping aside to allow their students to demonstrate their proficiency. This includes learning lectures, charges, as well as other parts of the ritual. It also includes coaching candidates and other responsibilities essential to the operation of the Lodge. This process is critical to the success of the model which will create a pool of brethren who are excited about their participation, talented in their ability to contribute, and capable of assuming positions of responsibility and authority within the Lodge.

A traditional progressive line begins with an appointed position, making selection of the appointee a critical decision held by one member: the Master. Although Masters generally do consult with the Lodge leadership – generally past masters – it ultimately falls to the Master to make a decision which will have a lasting effect, for good or ill, on the health and well-being of the Lodge for the next several years. Our mentorship model begins the progressive line with the election of the Junior Warden and, we think, addresses this problem by placing this critical decision in the hands of the Brothers of the Lodge.

Creating a pool of talented and interested brethren who have taken the time and effort to learn various positions and demonstrate their proficiencies through their work in Lodge creates another challenge. When it's time for elections, how do the members know which of these "workers in the quarries" are interested and willing to serve in what positions?

Our answer was for each prospective officer to express his interest to the Lodge by listing the offices for which he feels he is proficient and is willing to serve presenting that list to the Lodge Secretary. This would be done at the September meeting.

The secretary would then report at the October meeting identifying each position and all members who had declared themselves as being proficient and willing to serve in those positions. The members would receive this report at the October meeting and, over the next month, have time to consider their own thoughts and opinions regarding who is best qualified to serve in each position and then vote accordingly at the annual meeting to follow. Through their votes, the members would also express their opinions regarding the appointed positions, providing direction to the new Master as to how the members would like him to fill these offices.

Our collective opinion was that our blended system would meet the demands of training and identifying qualified men to be officers and leaders of our Lodge, while providing more freedom and flexibility to the Lodge and its officers. Our model provides an opportunity for anyone to become involved at whatever level he feels comfortable and capable. It also provides a remedy for some of the difficulties commonly associated with a progressive line which can interfere with the Lodge's health and development.

We at Arts & Sciences intend on using this system beginning in the fall of 2011 and thereafter unless the members decide to follow a different system based on their experiences with this model, and after further discussion. This gives the members the opportunity during the 2011 Masonic year to pursue their interests, learn new positions, and demonstrate their proficiencies. We believe that our experiment will contribute to a richer and more energetic environment for all of our Brothers to become involved in the activities of Arts & Sciences Lodge.

# Appendix 6

## From Profane to Master

by Chad Simpson

Arts & Sciences Lodge No. 792, in Hilliard, Ohio uses what might be called an expanded form of candidate education, which begins as soon as a man expresses an interest in becoming a Freemason.

A man who expresses an interest in Masonry is invited to dine with the Lodge. These dinners are held at a restaurant conveniently located near the Lodge and are held prior to every meeting. Attending the dinners provides the prospect with a chance to meet the members and vice versa. He is invited to attend the dinners each month. While the mechanics of seeking membership are explained by his potential sponsor either at or before the first dinner, becoming a Freemason is never mentioned again until the prospect raises the issue himself. He then follows the usual petitioning process but will continue to attend the dinners during this time. In fact, he will attend the dinners throughout the rest of his time with the Lodge - first as an prospect, then as a petitioner, and finally as a candidate and member.

Breaking bread together before the meetings is an essential part of the Lodge's culture and not only provides an opportunity for conviviality and fellowship but also provides a break from the concerns and stress of the profane world before entering the sanctuary of the Lodge.

Once a petitioner has been elected to receive the degrees but before he is initiated, he attends what is called a "School for the Profane," which is a one-on-one discussion session between the petitioner and a member of the Lodge with the goal of preparing the candidate intellectually for his initiation. The School meets monthly at a convenient place other than the Lodge hall in recognition that the petitioner is truly profanum – *"outside the temple."*

The first session of the School focuses on why the candidate chose to desire to become a Mason and a general discussion of the concept of Masonic Brotherhood. The second reviews operative masonry and the operatives' use of tools as symbols for life, culminating with the petitioner brainstorming his own symbolism for a standard set of Masonic working tools. The third session is a discussion of King Solomon's Temple and the symbolism of the spiritual temple. The final session takes place the day before conferral of the Entered Apprentice Degree, at which time the candidate reads Carl Claudy's thoughtful essay, *"Preparation."* Also included in the discussions are a presentation and review of Plato's *"Allegory of the Cave."*

Once a candidate is initiated, he is apprenticed to a Master Mason, whose responsibility it is to make sure he learns the traditional catechism examination lecture, attends Lodge when it is open on the EA degree, and visits another Lodge or two, if possible, to see the degree again.

Having graduated, as it were, from the School for the Profane, the new Brother now attends a Lodge of Instruction for Entered Apprentices. His Master Mason attends with him.

The Lodge of Instruction system is used all over the world as a method of teaching ritual and keeping the Work at a high level of quality. At Arts & Sciences, Lodges of Instruction are used as a venue for a progressive system of candidate education in the nature of informal, small group discussions or, rather, conversations held at the Lodge hall each month on the first Thursday.

The object of each session is to expand the candidate's knowledge of the lessons, history, and symbolism of the degree he recently received - and it is no coincidence that the others who participate revisit these same topics as well. The participants in each Lodge of Instruction include a discussion leader, two additional Master Masons, the candidate or candidates holding that degree, and more often than not one or two additional brethren. The Junior Warden leads the Lodge of Instruction for Entered Apprentices, the Senior Warden leads the Lodge of Instruction for Fellow Crafts, and the Worshipful Master leads the Lodge of Instruction for Master Masons.

We use Introduction to Freemasonry by Bro. Carl H. Claudy as the basis for discussion in the Lodges of Instruction. The book separately discusses each of the three symbolic degrees. In addition, we review important elements of the lecture of the degree being studied and we use the Basic Education Courses for each degree published by the Grand Lodge Committee on Education and Information as part of the Grand Lodge Apprenticeship program.

Candidates generally remain an Apprentice for three to four months, and a Fellow Craft for the same period, attending six to nine Lodges of Instruction before being raised. The first Lodge of Instruction in a degree is dedicated to discussing the candidate's impressions of the degree just received; the remaining sessions delve into Claudy's book on that degree.

To demonstrate his official proficiency in a degree, the candidate presents the usual examination "lecture" to the Lodge, but Arts & Sciences doesn't stop there. The fellowship at table before Lodge, the conversations and "back and forth" at the Lodges of Instruction, and attendance at Lodge itself are all part of the candidate experience and are seen as essential to the Lodge's future.

Furthermore, the goal of Arts & Sciences Lodge is to encourage its members and candidates to practice applied Masonry. Accordingly each candidate is additionally encouraged to write a short essay about some aspect of each degree that he found personally meaningful and applicable to his own life. The purpose of the essay is not to assess a man's grammatical, spelling or other skills as a writer, but to provide him an explicit opportunity to internalize some lesson of the degree. Though the lessons of operative and speculative Masonry are interesting, they are of little value if they are not applied in daily life.

By the time the new member becomes a proficient Master Mason, he has worked closely with ten or more members of the Lodge (his Master and three different Master Masons in each of the three Lodges of Instruction). This experience intentionally weaves him into the social fabric of the Lodge. It also prepares him to participate fully in the discussions which take place in every tyled meeting of the Lodge. And, as already mentioned, the Master Masons who participate in the Lodges of Instruction enjoy a further opportunity to engage their thinking on an aspect or two of Masonry they had perhaps neglected. Thus, they too re-weave themselves back into the fabric of the Lodge, and of Masonry.

Just as Apprentices and Fellows in Arts & Sciences are not left to themselves outside of Lodge, so also are they given special seating within the Lodge. Embracing a Masonic tradition adopted by Lodges of the 18th century, Entered Apprentices are seated in the Northeast, near the Rough Ashlar, and Fellow Crafts are seated in the Southeast, near the Perfect Ashlar. This ensures that every new member has his own place in the Lodge, and he notes this tangible change as he advances through the degrees.

Arts & Sciences limits the number of candidates each year which is unusual in American Masonry, but when a candidate requires the attention of ten members of the Lodge, particularly in a small Lodge, the Lodge cannot credibly work more than three or four candidates in a twelve month period without neglecting their duties to provide an thorough education in Speculative Masonry. However, the old adage of "working smarter, not harder" would seem to apply here. Why work as many as 15 candidates only to retain one or two active new members? Would it not make more sense to work two and keep two?

Ideally, a man approaches the door of Masonry with the sentiment that "something special" may be found within. While it is true that Masonry owes a petitioner nothing, an alarm at the door of the preparation room tells the attentive ear that outside stands a candidate to whom we have given an IOU for our future. Our responsibility is to redeem that IOU at full value, and Arts & Sciences Lodge's candidate education program is directed exclusively toward that end.

# Appendix 7

## On Being Master of Arts & Sciences Lodge

By Daniel D. Hrinko

### Ritual

As with all Lodges, the most visible responsibility of the Worshipful Master of any Lodge is the performance of the ritual. Arts & Sciences Lodge prides itself in excellence in all that we do. We value the importance of education and realize that our ritual is the foundation of the teachings of Freemasonry. Through our ritual, we introduce the Brothers to the symbolism of Freemasonry, the allegories, and the framework of the morality we pursue.

The Authors of our ritual chose the words and language very carefully to convey the images, ideas, and lessons intended to be the foundations of Freemasonry. Out of respect for our predecessors, we strive to be precise in our delivery of the ritual.

Words alone are not sufficient to truly convey the lessons contained therein. Using drama in the delivery or our ritual with careful attention to the use of inflections pauses and pacing will enhance the ability of the candidates to understand the lessons being conveyed.

To make good use of these skills, you need to have a thorough understanding of the meaning of words and phrases included in our ritual. This will allow you to choose the best manner for delivery to accomplish the goals of education. This will require a careful study of the language of the ritual and the ideas contained within that language. Use of supportive materials to truly understand each word, its meaning, and context is encouraged.

As Master of Arts & Sciences Lodge, you are responsible to set the standards for the rest of the Lodge. First and foremost is the need to set an example. Your personal skill in the work of the ritual is the model for the others in the Lodge. Therefore, careful attention to your own performance cannot be ignored. Polite comments delivered to others in private can assist with encouraging others to improve their presentation of the ritual.

You have the option to appoint a 'ritual committee' of individuals who are particularly skilled and well respected among the Brothers to serve as a repository of advice to assist in the teaching of the ritual and all related skills. This reduces the burden placed on you for 'hands on' instruction in this area.

The general expectation is that you be able to deliver at least one of the three degree lectures in its entirety and be thoroughly familiar with the others. This is part of the general expectations that you, as Worshipful Master, are proficient in all aspects of the work of the Lodge.

Particular attention needs to be paid to the opening and closing of the Lodge. This is the first action in the transformation of a common space into a sacred space. This is further affirmed by the text of the optional closing prayer in Ohio. In other jurisdictions, it is often referred to as the Charge to the Craft.

---

Brethren: You are now to quit this sacred retreat to mix again with the world. Amidst its concerns and employments, forget not the duties you have so frequently heard inculcated and so forcibly recommended within the Lodge.

Be diligent, prudent, temperate, discreet. Do good unto others as you would have others do unto you, and good unto all.

Remember that you are to befriend and relieve every Brother who shall need your assistance.

Finally, Brethren, be ye all of one mind - live in peace; and may the God of love and peace delight to dwell with and bless us. Amen.

It is easy to move through this porting of the ritual in a cursory fashion. However, due attention to this process will draw the attention of all in attendance to the important transformation taking place. Appropriate use of silence and a respectful manner will enhance this impression.

Our tradition calls for the Master to bring the light of a single candle into the darkened Lodge room following the silent procession into the room. This is to illustrate his role within the Lodge to "bring light" to the Brothers of the Lodge. The opening ritual compares the Worshipful Master with the sun rising in the east to "open and illume the day" providing light, guidance, and directions for the Lodge and the Craft who labor within.

The manner of entry is entirely up to you. Each of your predecessors made their decisions as to how to deliver the Light to the South based on their own thoughts and rationales. You are free to consider your own ideas on this action to make it appropriately reverent and meaningful to you.

### The Education of Candidates

As Master of Arts & Sciences Lodge, we strive to provide a thorough education on Freemasonry to all candidates and Brothers who actively participate in the Lodge. As has already been stated, our ritual is a primary means of educating our candidates and reminding our Brothers of the important lessons contained within our ritual.

In addition to the ritual, candidates are assigned a Master Craftsman who takes the responsibility for the education of each new Brother. It is your responsibility, with the assistance of the Lodge Education Officer, to assure that Master Craftsman are appropriately assigned to each Brother and introduced to them at the time of the completion of their Entered Apprentice degree. In addition, you are to encourage that the school of instruction for the Entered Apprentice are properly implemented by the Junior Warden, that the school of instruction for the Fellowcraft is properly implemented by the Senior Warden, and that you personally supervised the school of instruction for Master Masons.

## Craft Driven Features

Arts & Sciences is a Craft Driven Lodge. By definition, this means that the will of the craft, communicated to the Master and Lodge management, ultimately directs the activities of the Lodge. As a result, the nature of Arts & Sciences Lodge will evolve over time as the membership evolves. As new Brothers join, they will bring ideas, desires, and needs into the Lodge which the Lodge will need to accommodate. As Brothers move on due to death, geography, or other reasons, certain desires, ideas, and needs will leave the pool of active members making some activities less important if not unnecessary. This results in an organization that is constantly evolving.

For this Lodge to succeed across time, there needs to be a constant flow of information from the members of the Lodge to the management and from the management to the Brothers of the Lodge. Should Brothers feel that they are not being heard and have no sense of input into the activities of the Lodge, they will become disconnected, apathetic, and disappear. However, if a formal mechanism is created where every Brother has a voice if they are willing to use it and feels confident that their opinions matter, then they will be connected, energetic, and invested in the life of the Lodge being willing to take whatever actions are reasonable to contribute to its success.

Experiences tell us that are most important formal method of obtaining feedback from the Brothers of our Lodge is through the same discussion model with which we use to address other issues of common concern. At the annual meeting, it is suggested that a portion of that meeting be set aside to discuss the events that have occurred over the past year, the aspects of the Lodge that are most successful, attractive, and inspiring, and to entertain additional suggestions about ways of maintaining and improving the overall experience of Arts & Sciences Lodge administratively, ritualistically, educationally, and socially. These comments, ideas, and suggestions are the raw material from which the latest version of Arts & Sciences Lodge can be created during the planning meeting held in early December.

In addition to this formal mechanism of obtaining input from the members of the Lodge, it is your responsibility to remind the Brothers of the open channel from Brother to Master at any time regarding ideas, thoughts, and suggestions and that such feedback should not be taken as a personal attack or criticism of actions. Such comments are to be received in the spirit of ways to improve the nature of Arts & Sciences Lodge.

**Discussions**

Arts & Sciences Lodge recognizes that we are a Lodge of Masters of our Craft each with our own talents, expertise, and point of view. As such, we embrace an egalitarian form of education, that of the discussion. Topics need to be chosen in advance and the Lodge informed of them in to allow the Brothers to read, contemplate, and prepare their own thoughts on the topic of discussion. This process allows each of us to make use of our own expertise and evaluate the material being discussed through the lens of our own experiences.

The Master's role in this process is that of facilitator. An excellent resource for this process is the model presented in the book 'Socrates Café' by Christopher

Phillips. In this book, he describes how he was able to use open ended questions to stimulate discussions where individuals contribute their own thoughts and ideas to a particular topic. This book is highly recommended reading for those aspiring to become Master of Arts & Sciences Lodge.

One of the main challenges of managing a discussion lies in the ability to formulate open ended questions that lead in a particular direction. Discussions naturally tend to wander away from the original topic. Using carefully considered questions can bring the focus back to the original topic to assure it is covered thoroughly. Questions that are closed ended, or are answerable with simple statements, can dampen a discussion rather than fuel it. Participants will respond to opportunities to explain a statement, idea, or respond to someone else's comment when provided the opportunity.

A facilitator needs to be willing to invite individuals to participate to avoid allowing more vocal and assertive individuals to dominate the discussion. This may involve asking a particular individual to offer his thoughts or opinions rather than waiting for them to jump in on their own.

Unfortunately, as moderator, your own thoughts and opinions are secondary to your responsibility to facilitate the discussion. If you begin to express your own thoughts, your position as Worshipful Master will result in others deferring to you and your expressions are likely to suppress the life and power of the discussion. Therefore, you should keep your own thoughts to yourself until the appropriate time. You are free to ask questions that will lead to your observation being brought out by others. This allows these thoughts to be included in the discussion without the risk of the discussion stalling out because of the position you hold.

Timing is important. A discussion takes at least 5 minutes to gain momentum and 3-5 minutes to wind down. Therefore, careful attention to the time allowed for the discussion, the nature of the topic, and other considerations will allow an excellent experience to be had by all. Simple, didactic topics such as the exploration of a Masonic symbol, phrase in the ritual, or other similar topic can easily fit into a short time space of 10-15 minutes and be satisfying to all involved. However, topics that are much more personal, emotionally intense, or philosophically broad are best reserved for times when 30-60 minutes are available because of the difficulty developing the ideas, incorporating the comments made, and bringing some light to all involved.

Discussions are one of the qualities that define the character of Arts & Sciences Lodge. We strive to have such a discussion at every meeting contributing to our ongoing development of having meetings that Brothers look forward to attending.

As Master of Arts & Sciences Lodge, it is your responsibility to supervise the development of topics to be discussed based on the expressed interests of the Brothers. In addition, the overall development of topics needs to consider the expectations of the Grand Lodge Education Committee taking their expected programs and turning them in to expanded discussion topics.

You are to initiate the discussions, open the floor, moderate the discussion for civility and decorum, and keep the topic focused. Too much control from you and the discussion dies. Too little and it wanders from topic to topic becoming confusing. It is helpful to take notes of the nature of the comments being made and the ideas offered. This will allow you to provide an interim summary at the halfway point to refocus the discussion if needed. It also allows you to provide a thorough summary at the end summarizing the essential ideas revealed during the discussion. This summary allows you an opportunity to interject your own thoughts and opinions and bring the whole discussion to a close.

These discussions can be held in three different settings. Discussions that have a wide appeal and may benefit from outside resources can be held before or after Lodge meetings. These can include non-members and family members. Historically, this has happened twice each year and has been found to be one of the more popular events hosted by Arts & Sciences Lodge No. 792.

A second setting is to call the Lodge to refreshment to eliminate the typical Masonic decorum of saluting the East and other formalities. This can promote open discussion and exchanges of ideas. Some topics, due to the nature of the topic, can benefit from being held as a Lodge at Labor. This can reinforce the solemnity of the material being discussed and the power of the lessons being illustrated. This is particularly useful following the conclusion of the charge of a particular degree.

Historically, a discussion on the night where ritual is being performed involves a topic directly related to the degree and ritual just exemplified. This builds on the experience of the degree and allows an in depth exploration of some element of the symbols, allegories, and experiences of the degree. Such discussions typically last from 10-20 minutes.

Discussions on nights where degree work is not exemplified, the topics can be wide ranging and varied. This is where the area of 'applied freemasonry' comes into play where any topic can be addressed. It is important that, during the discussion, Masonic lessons and implications and the connection of Freemasonry to daily life is made. These discussions may last from 45-60 minutes.

Didactic presentation involve an individual with expertise offering an organized presentation to those in attendance interested in learning what this learned individual has to offer. These can be of great value when such learned individuals are available to the Lodge.

## State Of the Craft Address

An important aspect of Arts & Sciences Lodge No. 792 is the tradition of the State of the Craft Address. As Master of Arts & Sciences Lodge, it is your responsibility to maintain the "big picture" of the overall functioning of the Lodge. At the annual meeting held each November, it is helpful to the Lodge for the Master to deliver a "State of the Craft" address where the year is summarized with a special emphasis on not only those activities and accomplishments that epitomize the values of Arts & Sciences Lodge, but those important lessons of Freemasonry that are embodied in those activities and the ways in which our experiences of Brothers in Lodge have allowed us to improve ourselves as individuals and as a group.

This address serves as a "period" on the end of the sentence that took the last year to write. That summary also serves as the launching pad for the discussion regarding the ideas and goals for the following year that will become the beginning of the next sentence in the life of Arts & Sciences Lodge. Careful consideration should be made when composing this state of the craft address to reflect on those powerful lessons reflected in all that occurred during the past year.

### The Nature of Power

It has been said that power corrupts and that absolute power corrupts absolutely. Upon your assumption of the oriental chair of the East, you are by tradition and by code invested with significant powers which cannot be formally challenged except through the authority of the Grand Lodge. The ceremonies of installation convey honor, recognition, and everyone who is subjected to these forces ought to be proud of the confidence reposed in them by the Brothers of the Lodge. Such adulation and unquestionable authority both symbolically and by virtue of the code can lead to a form of intoxication that will contribute to disconnecting from the reality that, as leader of the Lodge, you are truly a servant of the Lodge.

The wise man always remembers that the authority granted through the position of Worshipful Master flows from the Brothers of the craft and that ultimately you are accountable to the Brothers of the craft. In addition, it is essential that you view yourself as a mere custodian of the Lodge and that, under your care, you have the ability to nurture or damage that life due to your actions or inaction. Such a responsibility is weighty and should not be approached casually.

When planning a the events for the upcoming year, the agenda of a meeting, or working with Brothers as individuals or in groups, it is important to exercise authority in a manner so as to promote the growth and development of the organization by including those to whom you are ultimately responsible. You should balance the desire to work quickly, efficiently, and to impose your own thoughts, opinions, and will on the organization and its members against the best interest of the Lodge in the long run.

### Social and Other Activities

Arts & Sciences is based upon the belief that Freemasonry is first and foremost the embodiment of the power of the individual relationship. When individuals have common goals, common activities, and common values, fertile ground for the development of important relationships is created. Our ritual, the center of Freemasonry, focuses on the common values of a belief in God in one form or another and the desire to improve ourselves by pooling our mutual talents and capabilities. Relationships founded upon such a basis have great potential.

Experiences have taught us that having multiple facets to these relationships allows us to build stronger, more durable relationships. Therefore, it is important to include activities and events to allow casual, social interaction. It is equally important to create events where we can apply our talents to the service of others, and events to include and expand our relationships to our significant others and family. Each calendar year should include several events both formal and informal that allow opportunities for these various facets of our relationship with each other to grow.

One example of an event that has historically been successful is a family potluck and open discussion meeting involving spouses, nonmembers, and guests. Having such gatherings in the spring and again in the fall has proven to be a wonderful opportunity to diversify the nature of our relationships, expand beyond the restrictions on activities imposed by the ritual, and to show those around us the activities and benefits of the Lodge. This has led to many men making a decision to seek membership in Freemasonry. This also gathers support amongst our family members for the time we spend away from them investing ourselves in Arts & Sciences Lodge and the practice of Freemasonry. Lastly, it allows us to benefit from the insightful ideas and opinions available from nonmembers and family members on such topics as seem appropriate for this setting.

### Planning and Communications

As Master of Arts & Sciences Lodge, you are the CEO of an organization with trusted associates who are willing, able, and should be expected to cooperate with you on the creation and implementation of plans, events, and other similar responsibilities. Therefore, your ability and willingness to communicate with the other officers is essential. You are to provide direction, suggestions, and request volunteers to whom you can delegate responsibilities for various aspects of the operation of the Lodge. In addition, you are responsible for providing support, training, and the development of skills for all the officers of the Lodge so each is able to make a contribution to the life of the Lodge in a way that exudes quality in our work.

This should be done through periodic communications among the officers in the membership such as emails outlining the upcoming events and the responsibilities expected for those events. Every meeting should be run in compliance with an agenda that you are to develop and distribute at least one week prior to the meeting giving the officers an opportunity to prepare their role in that meeting such as ritual work or other tasks. The same applies for events and activities.

A second form of communication is the planning meeting. The most critical of these usually occurs in the first week of December when all officers and interested members are encouraged to gather to discuss the goals, activities, and events for the upcoming year. It is at this meeting where it is decided the dates of degree work, many of the topics of discussions, and the long term planning for other activities such as feasts of Saints John, fundraising activities, social activities, and the like.

Periodically throughout the year, a meeting of officers can be used to evaluate progress, the successive activities, and to begin to shape any changes in the upcoming events. April, July, and September are excellent times in the Masonic year for these to occur allowing us to review the success of our inspection early in the year, the events that occur through the middle of the year, and to begin discussing the overview of the Masonic year as it begins to come to a close in September.

## Agendas

Like any organization, our Lodge works well when a plan is established that includes specific actions at specific times. One of our primary goals is to have meetings where people are glad they came and look forward to the next. This includes efficiently moving through those necessary activities permitting more time for those activities that we find desirable. Having an organized agenda, published in advance, and shared with all involved will support such a process.

Order of Business - The order of business can affect the mood and feel of a Lodge meeting as much as anything else. If, after a solemn, reverent, and powerful opening ceremony, we immediately launch into activities that are light, frivolous, or administratively boring, we have missed an opportunity to build upon that emotional connection formed between the opening ceremony and our true purpose of being in Lodge, that being to practice Freemasonry.

Experiences teach us that if our goal is to engage in a discussion that involves important issues and profound thoughts, that the proper portrayal of the opening ceremony will create an atmosphere of solemnity, a focus of attention, and a clarity of purpose that will support such an activity immediately following that opening ceremony. The same holds true for the exemplification of the degrees.

Therefore, experience should teach us that these important events should follow the opening ceremony so as to capitalize on the opportunity created by the opening ceremonies. Following the conclusion of the degree work or the discussion of the evening, administrative issues can then be addressed as the intensity of the evening can be gradually lightened before we are "exhausted." Such an order of business can contribute to that general feeling that attending meetings is a worthwhile investment of the time of our members.

### Committees

The use of committees provides an opportunity for focused discussions and problems to be solved outside of the Lodge meeting therefore avoiding such administrative concerns to interfere with the fundamental purpose of a Lodge meeting.

Committees to plan and operate events can be formed so the details of that event are worked out away from the open Lodge meeting with reports being made to the membership before and after meetings electronically. This allows such events to be addressed as part of the calendar of upcoming events and any actions necessary to be taken by the Lodge to be done so in a quick and efficient manner. Individuals interested in the details of such events are welcome to ask questions of committee members or volunteer to be on the committee.

A committee regarding the proficiency in the ritual work is highly recommended as this identifies a pool of Brothers who are known to be proficient and are respected within the Lodge to serve as a resource for new Brothers and officers to improve the quality of their work and presentation in the Lodge. This committee can also serve as a resource to the Lodge as a whole regarding various options available in the portrayal of the work.

The Grand Lodge of Ohio requires that certain committees be established and these are specified in the code. It is important to pay attention to these committees and recognize their existence and purpose.

In many cases, it is easier to do something yourself than to expend the effort necessary to identify a capable individual, recruit them to take on a responsibility, provide them with the support and assistance necessary to be successful, and to monitor their progress to assist in the successful outcome of the project. It is important to recognize that taking "the easy path" of doing it yourself creates to critical problems. First, you create a situation where it appears there is nothing for the other people to do and, therefore, rob them of the opportunity to take an active role in contributing to the life of the Lodge. Second, you create a situation where your time becomes increasingly taxed with day to day/hands-on operations of the Lodge resulting in frustration, mediocre work, and apathy when you feel that no one is working with you at the task of keeping this Lodge functioning.

# Master's Duties Under the Grand Lodge of Ohio

As Master of Arts & Sciences Lodge, one of your primary responsibilities is to assure that the Lodge meets all requirements of the Code of the Grand Lodge of Ohio. This includes essential requirements such as holding at least 10 meetings each year, portraying each degree at least twice per Masonic year (annual meeting to annual meeting) and that financial matters are handled appropriately through the use of an audit committee each year. These tasks are not exciting and can easily be overlooked when the Brothers are focused on the more attractive aspects of our Lodge such as the discussions. However, your responsibility in this area requires your diligent attention.

A thorough knowledge of the code of the Grand Lodge of Ohio is essential to your success as Master of any Lodge. The Grand Lodge of Ohio has made available a five lesson "course" consisting of multiple-choice questions pertaining to various aspects of the Constitution, code, and bylaws of the Grand Lodge. Pursuit of the answers to the questions contained within this course will cause you to spend many hours searching these documents. This process will contribute to a thorough familiarity with these documents allowing you to work more effectively as Worshipful Master assuring compliance with the rules set forth in the code in the operation of the Lodge. There is also a similar course of one lesson pertaining to the officer's manual of the Grand Lodge of Ohio with which you are expected to be equally familiar.

# Suggested Readings

*It is chiefly through books that we enjoy the intercourse with superior minds. . . . In the best books, great men talk to us, give us their most precious thought, and pour their souls into ours.*
**– William Ellery Channing, 1780 – 1842**

*The investigation of the meaning of words is the beginning of education.*
**– Antisthenes**

Those that have come before us have left us vast pools of wisdom from which we can draw our own conclusions and continue to support the development and evolution of Freemasonry as it relates to modern society.

Authors and publications of note include the following:

**Timeless classics:**

"Anderson's Constitutions of 1723", **compiled by James Anderson, 1723**

"Illustrations of Masonry, Second Edition," **William Preston, 1775**

"Freemason's Monitor," **Thomas Smith Webb, 1818**

"The True Masonic Chart, or Heiroglyphic Monitor" **Jeremy Cross, 1826**

"Encyclopedia of Freemasonry" **Albert Mackey**

More modern authors include Carl Claudy, particularly his series of books, *"Introduction to Freemasonry,"* his pocket sized tome *"The Master's Book,"* and his numerous essays often published in the *Short Talk Bulletins* from the Masonic Service Association of which he served as Executive Secretary for many years.

*"Idiot's Guide to Freemasonry"* **S. Brent Morris**

*"Revolutionary Brotherhood,"* **Steven C. Bullock, 1996**

*"Freemasonry At the Top"* **John Beaumont**

*"Masonic Action Teams"* **Robert Cottman**

*"Mackey's Jurisprudence of Masonry"* **Albert Mackey**

*"Our Station and Places"* **Henry Meacham**

# More Masonic Books Published by Macoy

The Craft and Its Symbol
by Allen E. Roberts
ISBN - 978-0-88053-058-3

Mackey's Jurisprudence of Freemasonry
by Albert G. Mackey
ISBN - 978-0-88053-026-2

Macoy's Worshipful Master Assistant
Revised by Allen E. Roberts
ISBN - 978-0-88053-008-8

The Builders: A Story and Study of Freemasonry
by Joseph Fort Newton
ISBN - 978-0-88053-045-3

The Lodge and The Craft
by Rollin C. Blackmer
ISBN - 978-0-88053-043-9

The Great Teachings of Masonry
by H. L. Haywood
ISBN - 978-0-88053-041-5

What Masonry Means
by William E. Hammond
ISBN - 978-0-88053-051-4

www.macoy.com